That's What
My Mother
Taught Me

and Other Ways
Generous Givers
Develop

HERB MATHER

DISCIPLESHIP RESOURCES

P.O. BOX 340003 • NASHVILLE, TN 37203-0003
www.discipleshipresources.org

Book design by Nanci H. Lamar

Edited by Linda R. Whited and Cindy S. Harris

ISBN 0-88177-329-8

Library of Congress Catalog Card No. 00-108423

DR329

Contents

Introduction

During a two-year period, over one hundred people sat down with me and described what giving means to them. Their ages ranged from thirteen years to the mideighties. They lived in Alaska, Arkansas, California, Illinois, Louisiana, Maine, Massachusetts, Missouri, New Jersey, New York, Oregon, Rhode Island, Tennessee, Texas, and Virginia. They included Euro-Americans, African Americans, Hispanics, Korean Americans, and American Indians. They lived in rural areas, in suburbs, and in cities. Some were relatively affluent; others lived on the financial edge. Most were from the broad economic middle class of America. Some were members of small congregations, and others were a part of large congregations.

During twenty-minute interviews, each one told me stories. Their stories described a pilgrimage to generosity. In fact, each person in this project was identified as a generous giver by his or her pastor or by a church business administrator. Being a generous giver was the only criterion established for arranging the interviews.

The people I interviewed taught me a lot about the relationship of giving and faith. They did not teach me with lectures or charts. They taught me through their stories. They described their spiritual journeys and how those journeys relate to giving. They tutored me by telling me vignettes from their life experience. I gathered insights by listening to narratives rather than to lectures. "Ah-ha" moments often came to them as they heard themselves tell their own stories.

I am still trying to digest some of what these generous people described. Each time I look over the transcripts or listen to the tapes of those remarkable conversations, I notice something new. This book is my opportunity to share the inspirations, insights, wisdom, and reflections of a sample of generous givers at the beginning of a new millennium.

I suppose you could call this series of interviews research, but it was not research in the sense of scientific sampling. Churches were not selected by any known, controlled sampling method. I simply called church leaders in a variety of geographic areas, told them of the project, and asked them to suggest a wide selection of congregations (size, settings, ethnic identity, and economic mix). I selected the churches from their lists in order to get a broad assortment of people for my interviews. Then I contacted pastors and church business administrators to find the names of generous givers from their congregations.

The research was anecdotal. You will not find any "R factors" in this book. Although I began each interview with the same question, the participants' initial responses led the conversations in a variety of directions. You will read words and phrases taken directly from transcripts of the recorded interviews. I intentionally weave my observations throughout the mélange of wonderful stories told by a fascinating assortment of people.

The Issue of Motivation

I regularly lead workshops around the United States on the subject of giving. Most of the time judicatories invite me to help local church financial leaders think through the way they encourage people to support the ministries of the church. Although I often accept these invitations, I may not always please the inviter. It would be easy for me to claim that the elements that motivate me to be a giver are the key factors every church leader should know. It would not be true. People are different. One size does not fit all. Human beings do whatever they do out of a complex combination of experiences and beliefs. In order to be a more responsible workshop leader, I needed to listen to the people in our churches who are presently giving, in order to discover the multiplicity of motivations that undergird their actions.

THE CHURCH IS TO ANNOUNCE THE GOOD NEWS OF JESUS CHRIST. IT IS NOT THE AIM OF THE CHURCH TO FIND THE MOST EFFECTIVE WAYS TO GET MONEY OUT OF PEOPLE. GENEROUS GIVERS ARE MOTIVATED BY INSPIRATION RATHER THAN BY MANIPULATION.

To learn about giving, I needed to talk to givers. It may be stating the obvious to say that more can be learned about giving by talking to generous givers than by concentrating efforts on those who do not give. Since approximately half of all charitable giving in the United States is through churches, the local congregation seemed to be the most appropriate place to learn about giving. In addition, my primary interest is in the giving that is invested in the mission and ministry of the church. Every generous giver has a story. Each has been on a journey to be where he or she is now.

My curiosity was stimulated by the stories I heard. Some of the people I interviewed were raised in fairly affluent families. Others were raised in poverty. Some were in the Pioneer Generation (born between 1928 and 1945). Others were Baby Boomers (1946–1963) or Postmoderns (1964–1981). A few were from the GI generation (1910–1927), and one youth was from the Millennial generation (1982–1999). Those interviewed grew up in a variety of geographical sections of the United States. A few grew up outside this nation's borders. Notable differences appeared in the stories according to family background and the generation in which the interviewees were born. Although different words were used to describe individual experiences in different geographical locations (East Coast, West Coast, Midwest, South, and so forth) and different residential settings (suburb, city, rural), few differences were noted in the stories. I mention ethnicity in the book only in those few places where the comments appear unique to the racial-ethnic group.

I wondered if different generations give in different ways. They certainly have different worldviews. Assumptions of a previous era in history may not be applicable today. Sometimes different generations seem to speak different languages. Even when they use the same words, their meanings may be quite different. An obvious conclusion is that the effective practices from the 1960's may not connect with twenty-first-century folks.

We cannot assume that a person's motivations are the same at age twenty-five as at age seventy-five. However, my observation is that age is not a determining factor in generosity. There are generous, giving Christians in each generational segment. There is one common thread among all generous people regardless of their age, economic condition, ethnic background, or theological leanings: All see themselves as people who share.

The Big Questions

Three questions emerged in my mind as I began my inquiry: (1) Why do people give? (2) How do people decide how much they will give? (3) What determines where people will give? I started my research by asking those three questions exactly as they were just stated here. The people responded to those left-brained questions with stereotypical Sunday-schoolish responses. I learned very little. The comments were proper and politically correct. People did their best to oblige, but it wasn't "real."

The questions assumed a common answer. Instead, there were many answers. In all likelihood, most of us are not aware of the multilayered reasons we do anything. Motivations are exceedingly complex. The way I worded the questions assumed simple answers, but the answers were not simple. The reasons for generous giving are what sociologists call "thick."

A change in strategy was imperative if I were to learn anything helpful in this process. I still wanted to discover answers to those three questions, but a different approach was required. I reworded the initial question into a narrative form of open-ended inquiry. The new question was, When you hear the word *giving* today, what experiences or people from your lifetime come to mind? Immediately, the people relaxed and stories began to roll off their lips. As they told their stories, the wheels of memory moved into high gear. One recollection led to another. Generous givers began weaving parts of their stories together—thread by thread.

Most of the people I interviewed had never been asked that question. The question allowed them to get in touch with their own stories. Their explanations unlocked some of the reasons they give, how they decide how much to give, and (in the case of these people) why they choose to channel most of their giving through the church.

This interview experience reminded me again that the faith we proclaim comes through stories. The word is not an analytical theorem but a story of One who came and walked in this world among real people. Gospel writers told the stories of Jesus. Luke and Paul added stories of the early church. Each person I interviewed had a real story. The stories wove together into a rich tapestry. Each story was unique, yet each contributed a valued stream of insight or a fresh glimmer of truth. The people seemed delighted to be invited to tell their unique stories.

I gave a similar assignment to students in a class I taught in 1999 at Saint Paul School of Theology in Kansas City, Missouri. Each class participant was required to interview four people about what giving meant to them. When the students reported on their experience, nearly all of them confessed their terror when they read the assignment on the class syllabus. Talking about the taboo subject of money with church people is frightening! When the assignment was completed, though, the students reported that each person they interviewed was pleased to be invited to tell his or her own giving story. The seminarians' positive experience of give-and-take confirmed my conviction that the problems with talking about money in the church are more related to *how* we talk about money than to the subject matter itself. In the assignment, the students did not ask people to make any kind of financial contribution; they did not even ask how much the people gave. The seminarians simply invited folks to tell something of their own spiritual journey as it related to giving. Their stories poured out.

Unanswered Questions

While the stories of the people I interviewed told me a lot about generous givers in our churches, they also raised many new questions. Early in my research I became aware of some of the limitations in this study. Many church members participate in our churches for years but never discover the joy of generosity. I did not interview them. I also wonder about the stories of people who are generous givers but are not a part of a worshiping community. I did not interview them. Some people never experience the joy of generosity inside the church or outside the community of faith. I did not interview them. I had neither the time nor the other resources needed to include those segments of our church and communities. I hope this study will encourage others to keep listening to the stories of a wider audience so that we may invite a growing number of people to discover the joy of generosity.

The Church's Involvement

Does the church have a primary impact on the generosity of people? If so, how does it make a difference? This study raises questions about how nurturing and teaching within churches affects the generosity of people. In each chapter, I suggest connections and ways for church leaders to continue this research in their own churches.

I tried to hide my preconceptions and pet prejudices during the interviews. However, every researcher brings his or her bias to the task, and I certainly brought mine. Long ago, political pollsters discovered that they could influence the results of a survey by the way they worded their questions.

The setting for the interviews can also affect the answers. In the case of this study, most interviews took place inside a church building. Did that location predetermine some of the responses? Did my posture or attire affect the answers? Most knew why they were coming for an interview. Did they have time to prepare what they thought they *should* say?

Although I tried to keep my opinions out of the interviews, my own theological and procedural biases are evident in this book. Even the choices I made early on in the process about the selection of questions have inherent bias. Even more so, my biases strongly influenced my selection of comments to pass on to you readers and the way those comments are arranged in this book. The reader will judge whether my predispositions distorted the witnesses.

Another difficulty with this type of study is that research, by definition, tends to be a rational act. Most generous givers are sensible, but the primary motivation for their generosity is not that they sat down with a financial analyst and determined that their act of giving money to a church was a prudent thing to do. They did not decide to become givers because of the data they pumped from a computer program. Generous people do not reason their way to generosity. They may carefully calculate the amount they will give and where

GENEROUS PEOPLE DO NOT REASON THEIR WAY TO GENEROSITY.

they will give it, but the act of giving itself is a wonderful mystery that goes way beyond simple rationality.

I am grateful to the General Board of Discipleship for granting me a three-month study leave to finish another book (*Holy Smoke! Whatever Happened to Tithing*[1]) and to complete the research for this book. My colleagues at the General Board provided both encouragement and space for the development of this work. Special thanks go to Mary Boyd, who has been my assistant for the past fourteen years. She graciously transcribed the tapes of the interviews. A group of readers made very helpful suggestions that strengthened the manuscript. I want to thank Lillian, my wife of over four decades, for putting up with my on-again, off-again single-mindedness when I get involved in a project. She deserves far more gratitude than I have ever learned how to give.

Finally, great appreciation goes to the people who told their personal stories of what giving means to them. I deeply treasure their candid responses to my probing and their thoughtful reflections. Their stories encouraged me. Bits and pieces of their stories are shared with you in this book. I hope you will find them inspiring as well as instructive.

I changed the names to leave the interviewees anonymous. References to ethnicity, age, or location are correct.

Endnote

1 *Holy Smoke! Whatever Happened to Tithing?* By J. Clif Christopher and Herb Mather (Discipleship Resources, 1999).

In Preparation for Reading the Rest of This Book

Individuals

1. Interview three or more persons using the following question: When you hear the word *giving*, what people or experiences come to mind that influence what that word means to you today? Listen to the answers. Your own experience and the comments of the people you interview will provide a framework for you to read the comments and experiences of the people described in this book.

Finance and/or Stewardship Committees

1. Assign each member of your committee the task of interviewing two persons with the assigned question: When you hear the word *giving*, what people or experiences come to mind that influence what that word means to you today? Plan to interview people who represent a variety of ages. Set a date when all interviews are to be concluded. Set a time for debriefing.
2. At the debriefing meeting, let each person describe the most interesting thing he or she heard through the interviews. List the following topics on newsprint. Ask for reflections about each of the topics.
   - Differences by age groups
   - Differences by ethnicity
   - Differences by economic class
   - Reactions to the offering in worship (regular offering or special offerings)
   - Reactions to pledging
   - Reactions to preaching on giving
   - What information did people seem to want about ways the money they give is used?
   - What do people think of the church's use of funds?
3. Ask: Considering what we heard, what are the implications for our task as a finance (or stewardship) committee?
4. Act on the basis of what has been learned in this process.

1

Is Generosity Taught?
If So, Who Teaches It?

Train children in the right way,
and when old, they will not stray.

(Proverbs 22:6)

The finance committee gathered at the church for its regular monthly meeting. Someone placed copies of both the monthly and the year-to-date financial reports neatly on the table in front of each chair. As the group assembled, one member after another silently looked over the figures. Two of them slowly shook their heads. Each one appeared to agonize over the precarious state of their local church's financial situation. Predictably, someone said, "We have to do a better job of teaching stewardship to children in our Sunday school." All heads nodded. Then another complained that "the denomination isn't putting out good Sunday school materials any more. They don't ever say anything about stewardship." Another member of the group nodded in agreement then sadly intoned, "Teachers just aren't as committed as they once were." Someone else said, "If people just tithed, we wouldn't be in this mess." The depressing commentaries went on and on.

There is probably a grain of truth in the comments made, but none of them hit the mark. In our desire to find simple answers, we look for places to lay blame. Preachers get blamed for not "laying it on the line" or, conversely, for talking too much about money. Sunday school teachers are blamed for not teaching children to give. Curriculum is blamed for not putting the right stuff in the class materials.

What kind of preaching, teaching, and experiences influence people toward generosity? Does Sunday school teaching make a difference? Do sermons? What difference do annual campaigns make in one's decision about giving? The assumption is that if we can discover what helps a person become a generous giver, we will know what to do in order to open the gates of generosity. All of us want to put our efforts where we can make the biggest difference. Doing that is much more productive than looking for places to dump our frustrations.

In all sizes of churches and in all parts of the country, I heard frustration about the lack of childhood training in the church. Everyone hopes that the effort and money put into the Christian education program in our churches produces measurable results. Is generosity one of the results we can measure? If it *is not*, there is no reason to blame the Sunday school for not teaching generosity. If generosity *is* one of the results of Sunday school teaching, then how can we do a better job?

Sunday School

Few people mentioned the Sunday school while recounting their personal stories of giving. One who did was a man from Chicago. Walter described a Sunday school memory as part of his early recollections about giving:

We had a little church [birthday] bank. You put a penny in the bank for each year of your birthday. That was so exciting. It just kind of stuck.

In Walter's case, it was not a teaching of the Sunday school he described but a drama that took place regularly and included everyone. In North American culture we ordinarily think of a birthday as a time the honoree receives gifts. But in this case, the honoree was the person doing the giving. However, the birthday child was also a receiver. The child received affirmation from the teacher, the other children, and the church for coming to another milestone in life, affirmation that he or she was important on that birthday Sunday. It may be that the most important thing a Sunday school can do for children is help them acknowledge and affirm that they are receivers. Each person receives the gift of life, and each is gifted in unique ways. People who can acknowledge being receivers are free to be givers.

Perhaps the most important part of Walter's comment was his observation that the birthday bank was exciting. Is *exciting* a word that would describe most of our Sunday school classes? The important issue is not what is taught, but what is experienced.

IS EXCITING A WORD THAT WOULD DESCRIBE THE TIME OF OFFERING IN WORSHIP AND IN MOST SUNDAY SCHOOL CLASSES?

In the same way, not many offerings are exciting in North American church worship services. The celebration described in Deuteronomy 14, when the offerings were brought to the Temple, bears little resemblance to the experience of the offering in most present-day worship services or Sunday school sessions.

Another positive Sunday school experience came from Judy, a Texas woman who spent several childhood years in England. She related an inner sense of obligation and responsibility to give to the teaching she received in Sunday school:

> *I think my Sunday school class, probably in the sixth grade, [was where I first became aware of] some of the teachings of Jesus, as far as being kind to other people and taking care of other people—that whole message. I was in England, and I could see what that meant more than I could in my own circle.*

As Judy told more of her story, she acknowledged that her husband had a greater influence upon her giving than her childhood experiences in the British Sunday school. Even so, we cannot discount the seed that was planted in her life in that class.

The Sunday school often gets blamed for a low level of church member giving. In spite of this popular complaint, none of the generous people I interviewed ascribed primary influence upon their giving habits to the Sunday school teaching they received when they were children. That does not prove that the Sunday school has no influence. It means that the people I interviewed did not identify it as a principal influence; it was not a major part of their stories.

Family Influence

Family, not Sunday school, seemed to be the most powerful influence identified by the people I interviewed. Many generous people were taught to be generous by their parents or grandparents. Many people told stories of parents giving them money to put in a church offering plate or Sunday school offering when they were children. A middle-aged man from California attributed his present giving attitudes and patterns to the power of parental influence when he said:

> *My mom would give us money and would teach us that was for church.*

We can only speculate about why early childhood rituals so quickly come to mind when people search for the roots of their own generosity.

Several people related stories of receiving church offering envelopes as a young child. Years later they could still remember placing a nickel or dime into the envelope every Sunday.

I have a similar memory from my own childhood. It is a mixture of positive and negative recollections. Receiving a box of envelopes as a young boy was affirming. I excitedly opened the box. A flash of distress quickly followed my joy. Right there, at the front of the box, was a special envelope. It was smaller than all the rest, and it appealed for a donation of fifty cents to cover the cost of the box of envelopes. I didn't have an extra fifty cents. If I saved up ten cents a week, it would take five weeks of offerings just to pay for the box. I felt "had."

I don't remember how my parents and I worked out the payment for the envelopes. I think they told me that the extra fifty cents was not an obligation but that the envelope was for those who could afford to contribute the extra. However, in spite of some momentary frustration over opening my first box of envelopes, the opportunity to participate in the life of the church through regular giving became an important part of my childhood.

Most of the generous givers I met during my research—especially those over fifty years of age—were guided into regular giving by a parent or another significant adult when they were young children. Many churches provide teaching and a box of offering envelopes to children in the confirmation or membership class when they join the church. A seventy-five-year-old woman from Virginia could remember the impact of that passage upon her life:

CHURCH LEADERS: SOME COMMITTEES ON FINANCE DECIDED TO STOP THE PRACTICE OF PROVIDING ENVELOPES TO CHILDREN BECAUSE THE MONEY THAT CAME IN WAS NOT ENOUGH TO COVER THE COST OF THE ENVELOPES. IS THE PRACTICE OF PROVIDING CHILDREN WITH ENVELOPES A COST OR AN INVESTMENT?

> *I joined the church when I was twelve years of age. I had offering envelopes. I may not have put but a dime in it, but I never knew anything else but to give to the church. I thought it was my responsibility.*

Some people who did not have their own envelopes observed the use of church envelopes and regular giving by adults in their home. Perhaps it signaled that "this is what you do when you grow up." A middle-aged man, whose seven children are now grown, said:

[The primary influence in my life was] my folks going to church and giving. They always gave an envelope. It just kind of stuck.

We may wonder about why it "stuck" with some folks and didn't with others. My interviewees were people who were receptive to the positive influence of their parents or other significant adults in their lives. There are undoubtedly many others who received similar training but did not develop into generous adults. I suspect that it is also true that a very small percentage of people who had no instruction or modeling in giving in their households have grown up to be generous people.

The Bible contains many stories of parents telling the stories of the faith. The primary place of teaching in Bible times was the home. In the book of Deuteronomy (26:5 and following) the parent recited the history of the Israelite people to the children at the time when the offerings of the tithes and first fruits were made. The recitation of history was related to giving to the priests, the poor, and the resident aliens. Teaching and example went together.

Teaching today is by example as well as by lecture or homily. A woman in her thirties from Tennessee recalled the Sunday morning ritual in her own home:

I remember every Sunday getting the envelope and my father writing the check . . . and my mother making sure that he stuffed it into his coat pocket before we went to church.

After reciting this family routine, she went on to tell of the next steps in her development as a giver. Jill said:

When I got my allowance of fifty cents a week, I got my own set of envelopes. I gave a nickel every week. So that was part of my growing up. We always tithed, and we always gave on a weekly basis.

The guidance Jill's parents gave through providing her with her own box of envelopes reinforced the practices she observed in the interaction between her parents. Instruction and tools (the box of envelopes) supported the family pattern. Her description sounds as if her inclusion in this pattern might have symbolized a rite of passage. I also suspect that Jill felt that she was more fully included in the family when she got her own set of envelopes.

M. Garlinda Burton, the editor of *Interpreter* magazine, told her childhood giving story in an editorial column:

As a kid, I received five nickels each Sunday morning to put in the church offering. My mother would knot it into the corner of my requisite cloth handkerchief so that I would not lose it.

My friends and I usually ended up with something to give, but many times, during the lull between the end of Sunday school and the start of worship, we'd sneak off down the road and spend a portion of those nickels on candy.

When we were caught, we'd be scolded about children in India, or people in Appalachia, or other people around the world who needed our nickels for food, clothes and education. The lessons stuck, and eventually I came to derive a sense of connection with children in other places when I put my nickels in the plate.

I never thought I'd see the places and people, but I was thrilled that God could use my coins to help people around the world.'

A young Texan with two small children expressed how her parents' example shaped her life when she said:

My parents had some bearing on [my giving]. They have always been generous givers; always participated in the church. I guess that is one dynamic that probably shapes us all.

A key part of Charlene's comments was the assumption that everyone else had the same childhood experience. Generous folks often believe that the key to getting other people to give is to help them remember (get back to) what they were taught as children, that giving was communicated as part of growing up. Unfortunately, many children did not have such positive role models when they were children.

A few people were led to generosity by a spouse, who had usually been taught as a child by a parent or grandparent. For instance, a retired blue-collar worker in Rhode Island described the impact of his wife upon his giving by telling her story. Arlen said:

My spouse has been the biggest influence [on my giving]. She lost her father when she was five years of age. There were four young children. She was the second oldest. Her mother was left with four small children. Way back then, there was no such thing as welfare. They relied on the church an awful lot. They lived right near the church. So when I met her, she was a teenager, and she was working. Her dedication was to give back. She has taught me how to give beyond what I would normally do.

Last week she wrote out a check to the children's summer fund. I would not normally think about doing that. I would think only about giving to [our own] children and grandchildren. But her thoughts are always to help anybody and everybody because she received so much help growing up.

I mentioned to Arlen that his tone of voice showed that he was proud of her, that his words resoundingly affirmed her generosity. Arlen laughed and said:

It makes me feel real good . . . a little upset that I didn't think of it myself.

Middle-aged people and older people were more likely than young adults to be taught generous giving through the church when they were children. In some families, the teaching was specific. Tithing was the standard. The rules were as clear as brushing one's teeth or washing one's hands before eating. A growing number of young adults who are a part of our churches were not taught to give regularly and generously when they were young. Church leaders know what to do when their task is to tap into previous experience and training; they tend to be at a loss when people with no such memory become part of the congregation.

When Church Giving Was Not Taught at Home

Pastors and finance leaders in congregations today rarely receive new young-adult members with clear-cut training in generous giving unless they are Korean. (We will address the unique perspective of Korean givers later.) For most people of any age, the giving habit came as much by osmosis as by direction. Givers perceived generosity in one or more significant adults during their formative years. A young woman in Texas said that her father was her giving inspiration. She said:

The person etched in my mind is my father. He was always taking food to people who needed it. He sang a lot of hymns and seemed happy while doing it.

Giving is associated with happiness in this woman's mind. The attitude of the adult seems to convey a powerful message. Attitudes probably speak much louder than words. This realization came to me several years ago while sitting in my office talking to a father of two young children. He mused about what he communicated to his children about giving. He said, "When the phone rings during supper, I snap at the person who wants me to buy tickets so poor children can go to the circus. I wonder what my rudeness communicates to my children about helping the needy?"

All is not lost simply because many young adults who join our churches were not taught financial giving as children, or because they have no memory of being taught. Many of these young adults recall how they observed or experienced giving during their formative years. They believe that they absorbed the value of giving more than they were taught giving. Watching the actions of an admired adult communicates a positive message. A middle-aged woman who had worked with the youth program of the church for many years said:

I watched my grandmother. She did not get very much attention. She got a pension check the first of the month. The first thing she did was put money in the church envelope. She used to tell me that she felt like God had blessed her more than she was able to give.

Grandmothers seem to have had a great impact on several folks. Kathy, a successful young landscape architect, said the greatest influence in her life related to giving was her grandmother:

She was the most generous person in every aspect of her life. She was such a joyful person. She gave a good example of giving of her self, her time, her talent. And she didn't have a lot to give moneywise, but she gave that too. She is probably the one who taught me what a generous spirit was.

Another key phrase in Kathy's testimony was "generous spirit." For the most part, generous young adults do not want giving to be simply a mathematical number. They want giving to come from within. True generosity is a reflection of spirit rather than of rational calculation. It is not imposed from without but is a part of a person's own identity and self-image.

WHAT EXPERIENCES OF GIVING AND GENEROSITY IN THE LIFE OF A PERSON CAN BE DISCOVERED? HOW CAN THE CHURCH BUILD UPON THOSE EXPERIENCES TO HELP PEOPLE BECOME THE KIND OF GENEROUS PEOPLE THAT WE BELIEVE GOD WANTS US ALL TO BECOME?

Grandfathers were not left out as people who influenced giving. An interview of a young adult layman at the seat of the Texas Annual Conference (United Methodist) brought the following response:

My grandfather did not attend church much. In some sense he became disillusioned with the church. But he always supported the church financially. After he passed away, we found the records. He had been giving every month, regularly, to the United Methodist church he had joined as a young man. There was a deep conflict in the church among the members, but he was not in it for those members but for the church. [The discovery of his giving] made a deep impact upon my life.

Church Teaching

Church teaching cannot be discounted. It did appear in several instances. An older woman in Los Angeles told of going to a district meeting of church women where the speaker gave her a whole new outlook on giving. Insight that results in changed behavior can occur while listening to a sermon or lecture; it just doesn't happen often.

A more common pattern is seen in the story of Susan, a young married woman. Her story is typical of several people whom I interviewed. They are among the millions of young Americans who migrated for employment. Before she and her husband moved to Maine, Susan and Ralph were involved in a large nondenominational church in northern Indiana. She described the preacher as "very, very aggressive about teaching the importance of giving." I thought that Susan's story was the exception to my general rule that preaching is not the decisive factor in causing a person to be generous. However, after describing her experience in the midwestern church, Susan went on to tell of an incident in her childhood that was a major influence upon her giving. She said:

Most of my training came from my parents—particularly my mother, who always taught me about giving, tithing. I just remember growing up, hearing again and again the importance of tithing.

Apparently the teaching of the church had fertile ground for taking root because of earlier training. Generosity seems to require the connection between childhood experience and adult appropriation. A major question for the church is how those connections are facilitated. Church leaders are tempted to get angry with people for what their parents or grandparents did not teach them. We wish that all people who united with our churches were like an older woman in an urban congregation in California. Gladys said:

I was taught to give and share at home with my brothers and sisters. It has carried through all my life.

Notice that Gladys did not mention specific church training. She did not talk about money in an offering plate. The testimony focused on her relationships with others. From childhood she was attentive to others within the family rather than upon satisfying her self-centered needs. Formative training in giving came at home and seemed to relate to family sharing rather than church contributions. It was after she grew into adulthood that generosity to the church flowed out of that earlier experience. Her "family" was now larger. It seemed to encompass the whole world.

Colin is a young adult from Virginia and active in his congregation. His relationship to the church had been hit-and-miss as a child and a youth. In high school he began dating a young woman who was brought up in the church. They enrolled in the same college and began working together in a faith-based campus ministry. He said:

I learned the importance of giving [in that organization]. I don't know if it was ever preached to me. It has evolved. We don't dwell on it.

Was it training, or was it osmosis? Was it teaching, example, or the inner working of the Holy Spirit? I suspect it was the combination of all three.

The Gift of Generosity

Perhaps some people are born generous. For others, giving may be a gift later in life. Paul lists generosity as one of the gifts of the Spirit (Romans 12:8). The most vivid example of a person who seemed to have the spiritual gift of generosity from birth was a woman from Los Angeles. Mrs. Janeway described her experience in this way:

As a child, my mother always told me I was too giving. I would give away toys, clothes, and everything else. Then I would go back and see about replacement. She always told me to watch out for my giving. I had a giving spirit. As an adult I give of my time to the point that I don't have enough for my family, and I know that isn't right. But that's just the way I am.

WE HAVE GIFTS THAT DIFFER ACCORDING TO THE GRACE GIVEN TO US: . . . THE GIVER, IN GENEROSITY. (ROMANS 12:6, 8)

I was fascinated by another California woman who said that she had no idea how she became generous. She could not ascribe it to upbringing, nor could she name any specific teaching along the way.

My parents were not churchgoers. My dad was not. My mother just kind of went— that kind of thing. I don't know how I developed such a loyalty to the church. And I like to give to charities such as the Christian Children's Fund. I don't know how I got there. But also, I like to give of myself . . . also my time.

Immediately her husband jumped into the conversation to confirm her self-assessment.

She really is into this . . . sometimes to the expense that I think is excessive of the proper distribution of funds. She gives a lot more of her time than I do. We don't have much of a conflict in that area. She just prioritizes differently than I do.

Is it possible that generosity is her spiritual gift? I think so. In Paul's letter to the Corinthians, he says that there are a variety of gifts (1 Corinthians 12:4). It may be that some of the people just described have the spiritual gift of generosity (Romans 12:8). They are people who have affirmed their gift. Even if that is true, I am convinced that there are other people with the spiritual gift of generosity who have never claimed it. Church leaders can help people discover this spiritual gift.

HOW CAN WE HELP PEOPLE WHO HAVE THE SPIRITUAL GIFT OF GENEROSITY TO CLAIM IT?

Intentionality

Most of the stories of parental influence that I heard were descriptive rather than prescriptive. A parental story that does not fit the mold came from a young man in New England. A unique word of counsel was given to him on his wedding day. The Rhode Island man described the advice in this manner:

My father said to me, "You know your marriage is involved in the church and you really want to make a commitment. What you ought to be giving is twenty dollars per week."

Many times parents assume that their children know that giving is important to them. They believe that their children will "catch" the idea of giving by simply growing up in a home where the parents regularly give. But generosity by osmosis alone does not seem to have the results that many parents expect. Even giving children money to put into the offering may not teach what the parents hope it will teach. Giving does not always develop out of those early experiences. A young parent from Texas is a good illustration.

My parents were always in church. I really never knew how much they gave. Never asked, and they never told me. There was always the offering, but I didn't know what that really meant. Mom gave me a quarter. It was not like I went out and earned a quarter, so I never really gave a part of the money that I earned. Of course, I earned money, but I don't remember giving away any of it to the church, not until I was married.

Giving is not accidental. It is not something that just happens. Giving needs to be seen in the context of the management (stewardship) of all the resources at our disposal. Parents want their children to grow up with healthy attitudes and practices related to the use of money. Many parents know that they are not setting a good example. They want their children to do better than they are doing, and they are open to receiving assistance in teaching their children about giving. The openness presents the church with an opportunity.

CONSIDER PROVIDING CLASSES IN HELPING PARENTS TEACH HEALTHY MONEY VALUES TO THEIR CHILDREN.

Some parents assume that participation in the life of a church will automatically provide that kind of training and example. For instance, a parent of younger children expressed recognition of the value of both parental and church teaching. She wants to provide Christian values for her children but acknowledges her desire for the church to be part of the journey. She said:

I want my kids to grow up with the experience of giving and accepting people. I was not misguided, but I wasn't guided either. I want to do some guidance for my children. I like to do volunteer work where the children can be involved so they don't have to figure it out all for themselves.

A New Situation

Teaching and example are both essential parts of the task of teaching children. A few people may learn giving by being taught. Most, however, "catch" it, and the lessons are reinforced through teaching. Nearly all of the generous givers I talked with identified childhood experience as pivotal on their giving journey. Childhood experiences may incline us toward generosity, or they may present a stumbling block. That fact became apparent to me a few years ago during a training session for local church financial consultants in the Chicago area. Twelve people gathered at a retreat center on Friday evening. At our opening session, each person told his or her own story of giving. In one way or another, every person told a story of being taught as a child to give regularly.

THE CHURCH CAN REINFORCE THE SPIRIT OF GENEROSITY THROUGH TEACHING AND ACTIONS.

During the Sunday morning session, the group of consultants-in-training studied 2 Corinthians 8. In verse 5, Paul described the generosity of the Macedonians: "They gave themselves first to the Lord and, by the will of God, to us . . ." One of the participants said, "Just a minute! Look at what Paul wrote. He said that they gave themselves before they gave their money. Friday night we told our giving stories. Every one of us started giving financially before we gave ourselves to the Lord. What is going on here?"

I was confronted with a question for which I had no answers. I turned to the rest of the group and said to them, "How would you respond to that issue?" After a pause, someone else in the group spoke up. "Well, the Macedonians were Gentiles, or at least people who lived in a predominantly Gentile culture. Most likely they did not grow up with the tradition of first fruits giving, tithing, and the jubilee that would have been familiar through Jewish tradition. It seems natural that they had to come to faith before they started to give."

That answer seemed to make sense to me. Heads nodded around the circle. Then a young woman to my right said, "That may be true. However, we have people coming into our churches today who are more like the Macedonians than they are like us." At that point the heads began to nod even more vigorously. Church leaders all over North America have observed that many of the people who are uniting with churches today have no clue about giving. In their frustration, church leaders often blame new members for their lack of giving. The Scriptures speak of people who were once no people and have become God's people. Church leaders can discover ways to help those who were not generous people become generous people.

When the Language of Generosity Is Unfamiliar

The question confronting the finance or stewardship committees in most congregations is, How do we communicate with folks who are not like us, who were not taught when they were children and youth to give financially through the church? What are we to do with those who have no memory of envelopes or parent-led Sunday morning giving rituals?

The good news is that most people were taught giving even if they never put a penny in a church collection plate. There are many kinds of giving. People who were not taught to put money in a church envelope each week still had experiences that communicated far more than formal church teaching. Unfortunately, church leaders, particularly leaders on finance committees, often fail to acknowledge any kind of giving except dollars and cents in a church offering plate. They tend to miss the interrelationships between giving of time, money, and influence. Generous young adults, in particular, seem to intuitively sense the interconnectedness of life. Time, influence, and money are not separate realms but are part of a whole picture of life.

Significant older adults who took the time to enter into a child's world had a profound impact upon younger generous givers in my study. For many young adults, time may be a more valuable commodity than money. A thirtyish young man in New Jersey responded to my initial question about what influenced his giving:

> *My grandfather. Just about every weekend he would take one of the grandkids to his house. He shared stories with us. We sat down and spent time with each other. He gave of himself.*

WHAT ARE THE STORIES OF THE PEOPLE IN YOUR CONGREGATION? DO YOUR FINANCIAL PRACTICES AND YOUR TEACHINGS ABOUT GIVING CONNECT WITH THEIR STORIES?

That story was similar to one from a twentysomething woman in Missouri. She said:

> *My mom, number one! My mom sacrificed a lot, I think. She stayed in a bad marriage for her children. Now I understand kind of what she went through.*

Another young adult told a story of a parent who gave of herself to keep her young family together after the father died. In all of these stories, giving has a much broader foundation than church envelopes and offering plates.

Implications

The strategy for communicating generosity to people who were raised in households that modeled generosity will be different from the strategy for communicating generosity to those who do not have that background. One way is not better than the other way; the two ways are simply different from each other. People who came from these varied backgrounds grew up in different worlds.

Many people learn prayers before they learn to pray. They recite nighttime prayers such as, "Now I lay me down to sleep. . . ." Or they offer a mealtime prayer such as, "God is great. God is good. . . ." In the same way, many people learn to give before they ever make a commitment to Jesus Christ. They begin giving before they know what giving is.

Many parents would like to convey healthy money values to their children—including giving. The church has an opportunity to form a partnership with parents and other significant adults to communicate a wide array of healthy and holy childhood habits. In a culture that sets its standards by economic accumulation rather than by justice and righteousness, the task is not easy. Many parents yearn for direction and support in their task. If they are generous, they may have no idea how they got that way. Many of them did not have good role models. They may hang their heads in guilt, believing that they are not good role models. They struggle to develop a new road through the desert of confusion. They hunger for direction and support in this important task.

Some people fear that teaching a child to pray or to give is manipulation. A good case can be made that teaching such habits provides the child an opportunity to exercise discernment as he or she matures, so that there is an honest choice whether to pray or not to pray, to give or not to give.

Not every child who is taught a prayer grows up as a praying person. Not every child who is taught generosity becomes a giving adult. Not every child who is encouraged to place money

THE PROPHET JEREMIAH BERATED THE SONS OF THE GOOD KING JOSIAH. JOSIAH HAD DONE RIGHT IN THE EYES OF GOD. HE SET A GOOD EXAMPLE FOR HIS CHILDREN, BUT WHEN THE SONS CAME INTO LEADERSHIP, THEY DID NOT FOLLOW THE EXAMPLE OF THEIR FATHER. THEY LOOKED ONLY TO HOW THEY COULD PROVIDE FOR THEIR OWN COMFORT AND ADVANCE THEIR PRIVILEGED POSITION IN LIFE. READ JEREMIAH 22, ESPECIALLY VERSES 11-23, FOR THE RECORD OF JEREMIAH'S WORD.

into a church offering plate regularly grows up to be a generous contributor to a church. If early childhood training is a form of thought control, the scorecard indicates that the practice is not terribly effective. However, a child is much more likely to choose to be generous if he or she has seen generosity modeled and if he or she begins practicing giving as a child.

It is true that an increasing number of people who unite with churches have no childhood training and experience in giving. Without realizing it, the church has depended almost exclusively on parental teaching about giving. When the parents don't do it, or when the parental guidance is not effective, plan B seems to be nonexistent. The church has a wonderful opportunity to provide guidance to parents about a whole range of disciplines, such as Bible study, prayer, and generosity.

Any attempt to communicate values in a capitalist society without dealing with money issues is spiritual malpractice. In many cases, parents have not worked through their own stories and convictions to discover and name their own values. The disconnection between espoused values and practice is likely to produce more guilt than helpfulness. The church cannot expect parents to teach healthy money values to their children if they don't have a clue about what to teach or how to teach it. In contemporary society, money must not be left out of the discussion about values.

Jesus didn't leave it out. He had a lot to say about money and possessions. Decisions about spending, saving (hoarding?), and giving are prominent in the Bible. The standards revealed in the biblical literature are often counter to the predominant culture in North American society. It is not easy to swim against the tide. The promise that the Holy Spirit is present where two or three gather together in the name of Jesus Christ is more than an affirming cliché; it is a testimony of spiritual survival. Slick fund-raising campaigns are not as important as helping individuals and families find strength for the struggle. That strength is found in community.

Some parents are benevolent people, but they fail to realize their own generosity. Culture's preoccupation with quantity of money and possessions dims the recognition of other kinds of giving. The widow who gave two coins in the Temple (Mark 12:41-44) would probably be discounted in our society and in many of our churches. Small gifts of that nature may have been casually dismissed in Jesus' day, too. Why else would that incident have found its way into Mark's Gospel?

Our culture tends to focus on shortcomings rather than strengths. We look for what can be improved rather than for what can be affirmed. Cultural values seem to discount generosity as foolishness. Accumulation is considered rational. This contemporary milieu presents the church with an enormous task of discovering ways to support parents who want the values of faith, rather than the values of Madison Avenue, to mold their children.

The good news is that many young adults are looking for ways to respond to perceived distortions in society. In the 1950's and 1960's, the countercultural movement dealt with matters of race, free speech, and war. The countercultural movement of the new millennium may be focused on money and the values of accumulation. The church has a window of opportunity to speak a word of truth and a challenge. The charge is to discover how to affirm the good things in the culture without blessing its dark side.

Church leaders also have the opportunity to develop alternative ways to teach adults who were not taught to give as children or who have lost contact with their early teaching. The people in my interviews tell us several clues about what the church can do. Many of the people experienced giving and sharing when they were children but did not go on to make a connection between those good experiences from their childhood and generous financial giving. Specific occasions of receiving that may have taught something about giving but have disappeared from consciousness can, however, be awakened.

A single-minded focus on financial giving cuts off the church from other important giving experiences in the life of the people. Every experience of giving and sharing of either time or money is to be affirmed. Whenever anyone has observed or experienced the fruit of the Spirit in someone's life, he or she has experienced giving. Every memory of good—whether giving or receiving—can be the opportunity for God to take us to the next benchmark of growth.

HELP PEOPLE REMEMBER THE GENEROUS GIFTS OF TIME AND CARING FROM THEIR CHILDHOOD.

As a child matures, he or she encounters both formative events and reinforcing events. It is rare for a person to become a generous giver without a formative influence during childhood. However, not all formative events that lead to generosity are church-related. The major challenge to church leaders is to find ways to relate the opportunity to give through the church to the formative experiences of giving and sharing in childhood.

Most of the generous people I interviewed remembered an adult who had had a positive influence on them at an early age. The sharing of time and interest was perceived as giving. When the church helps people remember those experiences and affirms the power of the gift, the church has an opportunity to help the people recognize and name the gratitude within them.

Church leaders have an important role in reinforcing healthy formative events and in relating those events to an adult world. There is nothing wrong with a child being a child; but when we grow up, we are called to put away childish things (see 1 Corinthians 13:11). The church has an opportunity to affirm the past without allowing people to live contentedly in the past.

Endnote

1 From "Reflections," by M. Garlinda Burton, in *Interpreter* magazine, Vol. 41, No. 7, October 1997; page 3.

To Put This Chapter Into Practice

Individuals

1. Write your own money autobiography. What are the earliest experiences you remember about money? Where did you get money as a child? What did you spend it on? Did you save money? Did you give regularly to the church? How did you perceive your parents' attitudes about money? Was money something they ever talked about? argued about? How has your attitude toward money changed during your lifetime? What are the biggest money issues you face at this time?

2. Recall times in your life when people gave you intangible gifts. When did people give their time to you? When and where did you see people giving their time to help others? If those people are still living, write a note to them to tell what that gift of time meant to your spiritual development.

Finance and/or Stewardship Committees

1. Covenant together to each write your own money autobiography. Spend a few minutes at the next meeting allowing members to tell about any insight they gleaned from the experience.

2. Invite people from the congregation to tell about their personal spiritual pilgrimage with giving as part of a worship service or in adult Sunday school classes.

3. Explore ways that your Sunday school reinforces the teaching that parents communicate to their children about money (including giving). Ask Sunday school teachers for their ideas of how you can help. Explore how offerings are received in Sunday school classes and ways to make that time more meaningful.

4. Evaluate your church's need for classes on financial management for various age groups in your church. Contact Stewardship, General Board of Discipleship, P.O. Box 340003, Nashville, TN 37203, or go to the website www.gbod.org for a list of current resources on the subject.

5. Develop special envelopes for children. One church provided envelopes with a pocket for money as well as space for the children to list ways they had given time. These lists were printed monthly in the parish newsletter. How can you, as a committee, reaffirm your commitment to assure that learning to give is a part of the maturation of Christian disciples in your church?

6. Consider how articles in the parish newsletter or in letters that go out from the church office can show the relationship of time, money, and influence.

2

What Has God Got to Do With Giving?

How does God's love abide in anyone who has the world's goods and sees a brother or sister in need and yet refuses help?

(1 John 3:17)

Is generous giving nothing more than a mechanical result of parental teaching and church instruction, or does God have something to do with it? Is generosity the result of nature, nurture, or God? Or is it a combination of all three? There is no way to prove scientifically that generous people got that way because of their early childhood environment, their genetic makeup, or special God-given gifts. We cannot put nurture, nature, and God on a scale and weigh each of them. To claim that God is a part of each of these dimensions of our lives is a statement of faith rather than scientific observation.

Suppose God does have something to do with generosity. The assumption forces us to contend with the issue of the nature of this God who inspires giving. Both theologians and generous givers in congregations affirm that giving is one aspect of the nature of God. The saga of God's self revelation as recounted through the pages of our holy Scriptures describes One who gives and gives and gives again.

The Roots of Our Decisions

There is no shortage of people who are ready to tell us what is wrong with us. We fall short and are scolded, or at least are urged to work on our weaknesses. We don't feel gifted. Why didn't God give us a beautiful body or a silver spoon? The consequence is that we may not even be grateful for our own lives. When a church makes an appeal to give based on gratitude, the communication does not get through to many. The connection between the good theology and the perceptions of the potential giver is lacking.

CONNECT AWE WITH THE ACT OF GIVING. RATHER THAN MANIPULATING PEOPLE INTO GIVING, ENCOURAGE GIVING AS AN INVITATION TO AN AWESOME EXPERIENCE.

This phenomenon is a modern attempt to relegate God to the gaps. That is, God remains God for us only in those places where we cannot explain what is happening with scientific interpretations. As science and technology expand their reach, the gaps get squeezed into smaller and smaller pockets. We turn to *Money* magazine or *The Wall Street Journal* or Warren Buffett to give us information on economics. The Federal Reserve Board will preserve our financial going out and coming in. Awe is in the latest econometric model rather than in the Creator of heaven and earth.

When culture consigns God to a few sidelines or mysteries that will one day be figured out, it is no wonder that the financial giving of generous people is often disconnected from spirituality. Is giving solely a matter of childhood patterning and/or institutional preservation? Many family rituals have their roots in faith, but the explicit connection easily becomes lost or hidden with the passing of time. Institutions (churches) are started and maintained for the purpose of glorifying God, but even churches can turn their attention to themselves and forget why they began. The question remains as to whether people recognize any connection between their giving and their relationship to God.

Perhaps surprisingly, young adults were much more likely than middle-aged or older adults to express connections between their Christian faith and their financial giving. They frequently and freely described how their giving related to their understanding of God. Although my question was about giving, Drew, a young man from New Jersey responded by saying:

> *Some of our friends are curious about why I believe in God to begin with. I think, maybe, if they had a better understanding of that, the part about giving would not be so hard to understand.*

In Drew's mind, his giving is related to his commitment and his witness. Perhaps he recognizes that Christian giving is primarily a response of the heart rather than an action of the mind.

Transformation

When people enter into a personal relationship with God, many aspects of their lives change. That is true whether the conversion is instantaneous or gradual. Many of the generous people who told me their stories described their growth in giving. One of the most articulate was an older Californian. Jorge said:

> At the beginning of my Christian life it was kind of difficult for me to be a contributor. As I matured in my Christian life, I became aware of the Bible and the teachings of the church about giving.

At first glance, it sounds like Jorge was describing an intellectual assent. But note that he began his life as a Christian before he knew much about what was expected. He had faith that hungered for understanding. He wanted to be fully a part of the Christian community. Jorge is a United Methodist. He may have been echoing the Wesleyan doctrines of justification and sanctification. It is not enough to say yes to Jesus. John Wesley claimed that a person needs to grow in the faith, starting with the acceptance of justifying grace. In his unfolding spiritual journey, Jorge discovered that giving was part of the whole package.

When the Bible speaks of "knowing" God, the references are neither casual nor cerebral. They are intimate. The Bible speaks of *knowing* to communicate a relationship that includes the whole person. In fact, the same word the Hebrews used to describe knowing God is also used to describe human sexual intimacy. *Knowing* is a word with many dimensions.

FOR MANY WHO ARE NOT POOR, A CONTRIBUTION IN A CHURCH OR TO A CHARITY IS A CASUAL ACT. FOR THE POOR, GIVING IS OFTEN AN ACTION OF INTIMACY.

In like manner, when young adults talk about understanding the faith, they mean far more than an intellectual head trip. I heard some young adults describing a connection between their lives and a mystery bigger than they themselves. In that sense, understanding is not a left-brained exercise. It is not a rational appropriation of doctrines as much as it is an internal "knowing," a verbal attempt to describe a mystical relationship of the person with God.

A younger Baby Boomer from western Virginia described his knowing/awakening in this way:

During the [capital funds] campaign, I was spiritual emphasis chair. It was an awakening. The process opened my eyes. Jesus became a real person to me.

In general, personal transformation is a much more important root for giving for young adults than any doctrine of creation. A doctrine is a human attempt to explain a profound mystery. Young adults want more than explanations. They look for and talk about relationships and connections. The connections may begin in small ways, but they proceed from that small beginning to encompass the world. Jesse and Donna are Native Americans living in California. They have had a hard life by most North American standards. Jesse expressed this connection when he said:

I have given my life to God and asked him to change it for the better. I am grateful that I have walked into these doors and have walked out with a different message. I have many more journeys now. And I am very excited about each one . . . so giving to me is God.

Giving means to me giving my time and all my skills back to the people. When I was growing up, giving meant giving to people that you like. Now that I am older, being closer to God, and learning a lot, I try to help everyone. I want to learn about the Lord. I want him to give me more knowledge. I want to learn more how to give.

Jesse's connections are with God and with other people. His remarks indicate that he does not separate these connections from each other. Perhaps that is what Jesus was getting at when he responded to a question about which commandment was the greatest by answering, "You shall love the Lord your God with all your heart, and with all your soul, and with all your mind" (Matthew 22:37). But he did not leave it there. He added, "And a second is like it: 'You shall love your neighbor as yourself.'" (Matthew 22:39). The two commandments are inseparable.

The Effect of Faith-Forming Groups

Several generous people that I interviewed associated their personal transformation with a spiritual formation weekend called the Walk to Emmaus.[1] A man from Chicago described the event's central role in his personal pilgrimage. He grew up in a home where church attendance and giving were part of the weekly routine. His grandfather taught Sunday school for about forty years. However, the focus of his life changed in 1991.

I went on the Walk to Emmaus in April. That really refocused me in my personal relationship with Christ. It opened up a real hunger I had of wanting to know more about God. As a result, I became much more involved in Bible study, learning Scripture, prayer life, all aspects of it. I think giving is part of that. Where before, giving was a means of supporting the church, now it is a means of worship.

Participation in this structured and intense small-group experience was identified as the radical reordering of life. It launched a new direction for him that included his finances. Generous giving had not previously been part of his pilgrimage.

A fortyish man from Virginia also affirmed the transforming experience of an Emmaus walk. In his participation he affirmed the changes taking place in his own life. It affected his understanding of God and his relationship to daily living. In addition, he saw that it made a difference in the lives of others.

> *I participated in the Emmaus walk and finally discovered what God was all about. That has been a turning point in both of our lives. My wife and I have both participated in that. From then on, it has been speed bumps rather than brick walls. That makes it a lot easier. It's been amazing to me the effect the Walk has had on people's lives.*

Gracie, a suburban woman from western Virginia, described her involvement in a rigorous spiritual program several years earlier. The "Ten Brave Christians"[2] program, or "The John Wesley Great Experiment," engaged participants for thirty days in the five disciplines of weekly group prayer, two hours each week given to God, tithing, daily personal prayer and meditation, and witnessing to others about their experience with God. Gracie said:

> *About fifteen years ago we did the "Ten Brave Christians" program. I started tithing then. We kept on but no longer count it exactly.*

Other kinds of intensive spiritual growth experiences were also identified as agents of transformation. Just as Jesus took the time to withdraw from his hectic routine and go up on the mountain, so many adults today have found their lives transformed when they participated in faith-building experiences that were a change of pace from the rest of their life. For many, the Walk to Emmaus weekend has created a whole new perspective on all of life.

A pastor from Florida led a workshop on young-adult giving at a national stewardship conference. A participant in the workshop asked him about the most effective stewardship program for young adults. He immediately told the participant *Disciple* Bible study.[3] *Disciple* is not a fundraising program at all. It is a thirty-four-week faith-building, small-group experience. Out of a confrontation with the One who is revealed in the sacred Scriptures, every aspect of life is changed—including the relationship of the participant with money.

Most of the young adults who told me their stories were quite clear about the connection between their relationship with God and their decision to give. This was particularly true of those who had not grown up in the church or who had been longtime dropouts from the church. Mark had recently started attending worship in a New Jersey church. A short time later he attended a huge Promise Keepers stadium rally.

> It was spiritually moving—got me motivated. And I have been giving a lot more . . . like to my family . . . giving a lot more of my time . . . and giving back to the Lord. And loving to receive. Once you learn about it and believe, it is tremendous—very powerful!

Although many young adults do not see themselves as receivers, Mark acknowledged that he had received a gift of love through Jesus Christ. His receiving was spiritual and his response was all-inclusive.

Mark was on a high after his Promise Keepers' experience and wanted to give more. Some might claim that a sense of guilt was the root of his inner urge toward generosity. If guilt was part of it, notice the nature of the guilt. He expressed his regrets, but he did not wallow in the past. He declared frustration in his pace of movement toward the future. Memory and vision seemed to be in a healthy tension.

Giving and Stress

Giving does not free a person from stress. When people make a decision to become more generous givers, roadblocks frequently lie in the pathway toward fulfillment. Repentant sinners still have to live with the consequences of previous decisions. The faith community is a key support group for most Christians. However, we are also a part of other groups who may not see life through the same lens that we do. A young man from Virginia described the tensions he has with his wife about the amount to give. They have two children, ages three and six. He would like to give more.

> The level of giving is always controversial. At times I feel guilty. I don't give enough, but I'm not sure where I would find the rest to give. My rule of thumb is that you write that check and then you make it work out. The two small children have lots of wants. I don't know how many needs. I think we have the needs covered. You know, we all have a lot of wants.

Hearing those words brings to mind the confession of Isaiah when he said, "I am a man of unclean lips, and I live among a people of unclean lips; yet my eyes have seen the King, the LORD of hosts!" (Isaiah 6:5). In a world of tremendous cultural pressures, it is not easy to make economic decisions that conflict with the dominant ethos around us. Generous givers, especially among young adults, look to the church for support of their newly found relationships and values.

Relational

Generous givers usually feel a strong connection with the congregation. Young adults in my interviews tended to be the most emphatic in their declaration about the influence of the community of faith. The church received them with open arms. They became part of a new family—the family of God's people. Their description of acceptance is more than a superficial act of hospitality. Acceptance is transformational. The love of Christ becomes incarnate in a group of people called a congregation. Gary Robards experienced the grace of openness through a little church he discovered in Los Angeles after he got out of the military.

Right away I found a very warm welcome. This is a very loving congregation. . . . Here I was welcomed with open arms. It was not long before I felt like I had something to contribute here. I give my time and money. I do it for the love of God. It brings joy to me. I don't necessarily feel obligated, but I really feel it is a joy and an important part of my life.

Gary seemed to intertwine his love for God with his incorporation into the congregation. The congregation provided him the channel to respond to God's love. Gary's experience may be a modern rendition of the attitude of the psalmist who said:

> I will come into your house with burnt offerings;
> I will pay you my vows,
> those that my lips uttered
> and my mouth promised when I was in trouble.
> I will offer to you burnt offerings of fatlings,
> with the smoke of the sacrifice of rams;
> I will make an offering of bulls and goats.
> Come and hear, all you who fear God,
> and I will tell what he has done for me.
> (Psalm 66:13-16)

Psalm 66 begins with a hymn of praise for the creation. Then it moves to a recital of the exodus event. After the affirmation of God's creation and God's act of redemption, the psalmist expresses thanksgiving through sacrifices and offerings. In much the same way, the offering is an act of worship that connects the worshiper with the One who creates and redeems. The worshiper looks upon the great events of creation and redemption as part of his or her life right now. Past events are part of present reality. What God has done for the whole community of faith through human history requires a response—now. The Temple culture provided the psalmist a means of response, the burnt offerings of a ritual sacrifice.

Offerings in a worship service have to be more than paying the bills if generous giving is to be part of the experience of contemporary Christian people. Many generous Christians experience giving as a means to connect with the Holy One. This is amazing when we consider how rarely church leaders overtly work at helping people make the connection. People are going to find a way to express their relationship with God. An issue for the church is whether the institution will be a stumbling block or a means of connection.

Generous givers (particularly young adults) did not deny the hard-nosed pragmatic elements of operating the institutional church, but they insisted that there is more to giving than supporting the organization. Faith has both human and spiritual dimensions, and neither aspect is separate from the real world of earning a living, raising a family, and learning to live with neighbors.

How Church Giving Is Different

Throughout the history of the Christian church, people have struggled with the delicate balance between affirming the connection between God and the world and the call to distinguish between the ways of the world and the will of God. The issue is often expressed by paraphrasing John 17: How do we live *in* the world without being *of* the world? A young adult from New Jersey wanted to affirm a differentiation between the practices of the church and what he saw in the world of commerce. Mike said:

> In the business world you may have fourteen different ways to raise money. Let's keep [church giving] focused on spiritual growth. I have to share that with people and what it is doing in my life. As a Christian, I want to spread the gospel. Equipping the saints might be a good place to start. Christ washing the feet of his disciples is about giving.

Generous Christians do not wish to withdraw from the world. Instead, they want their relationship with Jesus Christ to affect their relationships in the home, office, and every other dimension of life. The young adults I interviewed expressed this certitude most directly. If we have a personal relationship with Christ, new relationships with people will develop. We do not always recognize that the new relationship with Christ developed within a faith community. The Holy Spirit works within and through community. Furthermore, the impulse to share is nurtured within community.

COMMUNICATE THE DISTINCTION BETWEEN WORSHIP AND SECULAR LIFE WITHOUT FALLING INTO THE PIT OF NAMING TWO REALMS THAT HAVE NOTHING TO DO WITH EACH OTHER. PARALLEL PATHS THAT NEVER TOUCH SOON FORGET THAT THE OTHER IS THERE.

At times, the faith journey is inward. For some, the connection with God could not be expressed within the church building. A connection with God means a connection with the hurts of the world. After her first husband died at a young age, Mildred married a former Catholic seminarian. Each partner in this marriage brought a strong inner sense of a calling to make a difference in the world. Mildred had the conviction that this calling was an expression of her faith. She articulated her perspective in this manner.

I am a firm believer that funds follow faith. The bottom line: Those who believe, give. Why we give as much as we do here is the mission outreach in the city. It is particularly important to reach the youth. We have the answers. If we don't tell them about it, they will never know.

It seems doubtful that Mildred could conceive of faith that does not express itself in reaching out to others. A person must have a center in order to invest his or her funds in ways that work for significant change in the world.

Giving From the Heart

If we think we have received nothing from God, why would we bother to respond out of gratitude? From the Christian perspective, until we recognize and affirm the gift of God's love and forgiveness in Jesus Christ, we cannot respond in gratitude. When we are convinced that we earned everything we have that is worthwhile, there is no basis for gratitude. Where there is generosity, there is conviction. Where there is generosity, there is enthusiasm. Conviction and enthusiasm emerge from what God has done and is doing in the life of the giver. Generous giving is a response. Unless this connection between God's love and the lives of the people of the church is acknowledged, the church is unlikely to see the evidences of generosity. The testimonies of generous givers resemble the affirmation expressed in Psalm 7:17:

THE STARTING POINT FOR GENEROUS GIVING IS NOT A SLICKER CAMPAIGN; IT IS CONVERSION.

> I will give to the LORD the thanks due to his righteousness,
> and sing praise to the name of the LORD, the Most High.

Generous people today know that their giving is going through an institution (the church), yet it is an act made in response to the Word of God and the work of God in their lives and in the world.

Over and over again, I heard generous people speak of giving coming from their hearts more than from their pocketbooks. When giving is a heart issue, it is all-encompassing. Giving is a tangible act, but it is neither a performance for the crowd nor an action taken to obtain a brief spiritual high. Giving from the heart is more than sentimentality. A California woman used an interesting analogy to describe how heart giving and duty are intertwined:

> It's like decorating the seasons. Christmas and Easter are big. And that is sometimes a three- or four-hour job. We try to do it one Saturday. There is some enjoyment in knowing that you are making everybody else's celebration of Easter/Christmas— whatever the season is—that much more meaningful for them. You get some joy out of that. And some of it is duty. Having been a member of this congregation as long as we have, it's like giving back—a little bit of duty to fill in where people are not able. They have moved away, died, or just are unable to do it. It's like it's our term to step in and do it.

Generosity is multidimensional. It relates the giver to God, to the community of faith, and to the world outside the institution. Ellen, an elderly woman in Virginia, may have been a little judgmental, but she got at the same point. In strongly affirming the need for integrity in giving, she asserted a connection between giving and God while expressing little patience with some contemporary expressions of religion. She said:

> A lot of young people get into [financial] problems. The first thing they do is join some religious sect. They come down with glorious expressions on their face and walk around like they are in a trance. They have to realize that a mountaintop experience may be all right, but you have to come down and live in the real world. There is no easy way to be a Christian.

If Ellen is correct in her observation, financial problems are in some cases the catalyst for people to turn to God. People in trouble often reach out to someone or something. The taboo about speaking of money in the church has created a barrier for too many people. Congregations have an opportunity to be available with the love of Christ as well as practical help and the emotional support of a faith community.

The congregation's task is to receive people wherever they are in their spiritual journey. But the mission is not to leave them at the starting line. Acceptance includes helping people develop appreciation for and acceptance of God's love. Their response to acceptance by God is meant to be all-encompassing. Inclusion involves both the large-scale issues of justice and the environment as well as the micro issues of how we deal with money. The desired end is transformation—a new heaven and a new earth as well as becoming new people (see 1 Peter 2:9-10). Making disciples of Jesus Christ is far more than adding a person's name to the membership roster of a church.

The biblical witness repeatedly notes that the relationship of a person to his or her possessions is a reflection of the person's relationship with God. Giving is only one dimension of the picture, but it is an important element. For some, it may be the pivotal element.

Spiritual dimensions and financial dimensions intertwine. Few people can give generously unless they have the rest of their financial life in order. For many, there is too much month left at the end of the money. However, most people have difficulty getting their financial life in order unless they have their life together. The people I interviewed who seemed to integrate giving into their whole life could point to a time or a person who helped them see the connections. A man from Tennessee told of an incident on his eighteenth birthday. Saul's grandmother was the matriarch of the family and had a talk with him on the threshold of his entry into adulthood. She said:

> I want to share a special secret with you. Since you were a child your mother and your father taught you to tithe to the church and to God. Right now I want to tell you why it is that we do that. She paused for a moment. She looked up at the sky. And she said, "Our God, our heavenly Father, is the owner and ruler of this vast universe. He does not need our money. But I will tell you this, when we give God the very first of our very best, we fill God's heart with joy."

It seems clear that for Saul, the issue was not what we can get God to do for us but what we can do to bring joy to God. Saul's grandmother shared her wisdom with him at a receptive moment in his life. She gave the rationale. That message often falls on deaf ears because it is so countercultural. But when we use the gimmicks of the culture rather than invite people to serve Yahweh, we sell out to the cultural gods.

We are not called to make God in our image; we affirm that humanity is made in God's image. And what is that image? When the writer of 1 John wrote about love, he proclaimed, "In this is love, not that we loved God but that he loved us and sent his Son to be the atoning sacrifice for our sins" (1 John 4:10). In other words, God is a giver. What God gives is love. That gift is seen most dramatically in the person of Jesus. Although God is described as a giver in many places in the Bible, the summary of God's giving is the statement in John 3:16 that "God so loved the world that he gave . . ." In this affirmation, the root of all giving is God's grace.

Church financial giving usually sails under the verbal flag of stewardship. Although giving out of our economic abundance is part of the Christian's stewardship, it is not the whole. When church leaders request a workshop or seminar on stewardship, I can be confident that they want to discover some ways to increase giving. Whenever a workshop or seminar is presented on stewardship theology, you can count on hearing a classic description rooted in a theology of creation. The focus is almost always on the Old Testament, especially Genesis 1–3 and psalms such as Psalm 24. In the usual formulation, we describe the theological base as

1. God made it all.
2. Everything we have is a gift.
3. We can't take it with us.
   Therefore,
4. Our task is to manage the gift out of gratitude.

In this formulation, theologians usually turn to the beginning of the Hebrew Bible. In both of the Genesis Creation stories, the Creator God spoke the heavens and the earth into being. The psalmist poetically affirmed God as the one who made it all in the beautiful Hebraic poetry of Psalm 104:

> You stretch out the heavens like a tent . . .
> You set the earth on its foundations . . .
> O LORD, how manifold are your works!
> In wisdom you have made them all;
> the earth is full of your creatures.
>
> (Psalm 104:2b, 5, 24)

A similar song of praise is offered in the nineteenth psalm:

> The heavens are telling the glory of God;
> and the firmament proclaims his handiwork.
>
> (Psalm 19:1)

The psalmist had no question about who owned it all when the twenty-fourth psalm was penned:

> The earth is the LORD's and all that is in it,
> the world, and those who live in it.
>
> (Psalm 24:1)

A sense of awe and gratitude flows from these passages like water coming from a fountain. The writer expresses a reverence for the created world and the power of the One who created it. The recognition that we bring nothing into the world and take nothing out of the world at our death is meant to affirm God's ultimate and total ownership.

Few church members argue with this theological affirmation. At the same time, it is difficult to communicate a sense of awe about God's creation in this modern world. Headlines are reserved for technological marvels and athletic prowess. We live in an urban world of concrete and television and cyberspace. In contrast, the poetry of Genesis and the Psalms was developed in an agrarian world when life expectancy was short. Life was precarious, and everyone knew it. Today we read predictions that people will soon be able to live relatively healthy lives until they are around 150 years of age. Although there are many serious diseases, we keep on believing that scientific breakthroughs will soon conquer them and that illness, accident, and disease will only afflict "the other guy."

A few ecologists and a dwindling number of farmers join church steward-ship leaders to keep alive the affirmations of creation theology. Believers hardly ever argue with it, but an urbanized North American is rarely inspired to put money in a collection plate on the basis of sound creation theology. Such was not the case during most of the nineteenth century and the first half of the twentieth century.

I grew up on a farm in southern Minnesota. The creation was the basis for our livelihood. We knew that our eighty acres were blessed with rich soil. We also knew that the rich soil and our hard work did not guarantee a crop. The weather was the wild card. Too much rain, too little rain, or rain at the wrong times could mean economic disaster. We were concerned about an unusually late frost in the spring or an early freeze in the fall. Although we did not live with a sense of helplessness, we were well aware that many factors were outside of our control.

Life is different today. For most of us, bad weather is an inconvenience rather than a matter of survival. We look for technological fixes for the problems of the world rather than recognizing our dependency on the Cre-ator of heaven and earth.

Creation theology assumes a sense of awe and gratitude. Awe is more likely to be expressed today over the athletic prowess of a Michael Jordan than over a starry night. Our jaws drop open when looking at a huge, new building, but many of us fail to notice the flower that comes up through a crack in the sidewalk. A lack of gratitude is rampant in our culture. Fifty years ago a popular song claimed that the best things in life are free. I won-der if lyrics that put forward such a claim could make the charts today.

When it comes to economics, gratitude is rare. There may be a momen-tary sense of joy at a Christmas bonus, but it quickly passes. In fact, instead of feeling grateful, many of us feel like we deserve far better than we have received. Paul's analogy that "to one who works, wages are not reckoned as a gift but as something due" (Romans 4:4) is probably affirmed more vigor-ously today than it ever has been in history. Many take it a step further to claim that getting rich is their due. Paul's comment was an illustration of grace. We have separated giving from grace.

A few of the people I interviewed did tip their hat in the direction of the doctrine of creation when they used the cliché, You can't take it with you. However, even in those instances, the doctrine seemed to be a rationaliza-tion of their own generosity rather than a motivation for their giving.

Between the lines of the interviews, I heard an aversion to secular fundraising devices. Instead, there was the deep sense of a personal call of God upon the people's lives—including their money. Giving money must not be separated from a call to give oneself. None of the interviewees quoted Philippians 2:5-11, but it is possible to hear the message of that lyric passage in their comments.

> Let the same mind be in you that was in Christ Jesus,
> who, though he was in the form of God,
>> did not regard equality with God
>> as something to be exploited,
> but emptied himself,
>> taking the form of a slave,
>> being born in human likeness.
> And being found in human form,
>> he humbled himself
>> and became obedient to the point of death—
>> even death on a cross.
> Therefore God also highly exalted him
>> and gave him the name
>> that is above every name
> so that at the name of Jesus
>> every knee should bend,
>> in heaven and on earth and under the earth,
> and every tongue should confess
>> that Jesus Christ is Lord,
>> to the glory of God the Father.
>
> (Philippians 2:5-11)

Endnotes

1 For further information about the Walk to Emmaus, contact The Upper Room, P.O. Box 340003, Nashville, TN 37203-0004; phone 615-340-7200; www.upper-room.org.

2 This program of the General Board of Discipleship was originally called "Wanted: Ten Brave Christians." Two components of the program packet were *The John Wesley Great Experiment* booklet and *A Life That Really Matters*, published by Tidings/Discipleship Resources. They are out of print by Discipleship Resources but are now available through spiritslaughing.com.

3 For information on *Disciple* Bible study, contact The United Methodist Publishing House, 201 Eighth Avenue, South, Nashville, TN 37203; phone 1-800-672-1789; www.umph.com.

To Put This Chapter Into Practice

Individuals

1. List the ways in which you relate your financial giving to your understanding of God.
2. During the next worship service, consciously focus on ways in which the offering helps you connect with God.
3. Read Matthew 25:31-46. How does your giving fulfill the "did it to one of the least of these" dimensions of relationship to God?

Finance and/or Stewardship Committees

1. Look over recent letters and newsletter articles you sent to the people of your congregation. What references were made to the connection between God and giving? In what ways are your messages about giving different from the messages of secular fundraising?
2. If you send monthly or quarterly financial statements, do these statements help people see that their giving is part of God's love, mercy, and justice in the world?
3. Stop using the rational doctrine of creation as the primary rationale (or argument) for urging people to give. Help people experience and name the connection between ways they have received throughout their lives and the transforming gift of love in Jesus Christ. Offer classes on the relationship of giving and faith to the people of your congregation.
4. Develop a system for communicating with new members and those who are considering membership in the church. Instead of giving them only facts and figures, tell them the meaning (give a testimony) about the way giving is an expression of faith in Jesus Christ.
5. Pray for one another on your committee, that each person's giving might more fully be an act of gratitude flowing from what God has done for us and in us through the gift of love in Jesus Christ.

3

Peer Pressure and the Impact of the Community

Let your light shine before others, so that they may see your good works and give glory to your Father in heaven.

(Matthew 5:16)

Two significant questions arise when we consider the influence of peers upon giving. The first question is, Are generous givers, in fact, influenced by peers to give generously? There is a mantra in secular fundraising that "people give to people," not to organizations or to budgets or to ideas. Does this theory hold true for those who give through the church?

If the hypothesis is true, the second question becomes an ethical one. Is it appropriate for church leaders to use peer influence to encourage greater generosity? Can peer influence be used without becoming manipulative? Is a personal witness about one's giving a subtle (or not so subtle) means to pry money out of a friend's pocketbook?

Neither casual observers nor sociological experts deny that people influence other people. Advertisers scramble to sign up famous athletes to promote their products. Nike paid Michael Jordan millions of dollars because they believed that his name would influence potential buyers to purchase their athletic shoes. Corporations hire lobbyists to influence elected officials to pass laws that will enhance the sales and distribution of their products or services. One of the first things an effective lobbyist must do is make friends with the legislators. Without personal relationships there is little influence.

Parents generally believe in the power of peer influence. They don't want their children running with "the wrong crowd." Children are influenced to wear certain clothes, to buy certain records, and to be seen with specific peer leaders. The question is not whether children are influenced by peers but *which* peers will influence the children.

United States presidents have been sullied by a breach of trust from cabinet members or senior advisors. An old cliché announces, With friends like that, who needs enemies? The power of good and bad influences seems self-evident.

Evidence From Generous Givers

I looked for evidence in the interviews of peer communication being, or not being, an important factor in the generosity of the interviewees. I found that the data does not supply clear-cut answers to the question. Few of the interviewees directly attributed their generosity to the influence of a peer— except for a spouse.

A vivid story about the influence of a spouse came from a young couple in New Jersey. Dean grew up in a lower middle class home with parents who were involved in the community as well as in the church. The recollections Dean spoke of were about the efforts that went into coaching sports and involvement with other community organizations. He believes that his generosity was strongly influenced by his parents. His wife, Sally, however, discovered generosity through Dean. She said:

I had just the opposite [experience growing up]. My parents were always working. And they would come here, but they never volunteered anything. Dean taught me a lot about giving—not just by teaching but by seeing something in him that I really missed as a child.

Another description of the influence of a spouse came from Kermit. He said:

My wife was always giving. It seemed strange to me. However, I found myself gradually falling into giving.

Kermit seems to have learned giving by osmosis, a unique form of peer influence. He went on to describe how his wife's influence had been enhanced by the church's ministry to him after an auto accident, by the personal witness of a golfing friend, and by the support of choir members in the congregation. Each of these is a form of peer influence.

Many testimonies by generous givers tell of something missing in their personal life that was filled when they began to give. Giving was a part of

Dean's life as a child. The church gave him the opportunity to channel that giving into the community and the world. Sally found a similar context for her newly discovered joy of giving.

Cedric, a young financial planner in New Jersey, has only been back in the church for four years. He described the corporate peer influence of a church youth group. It was not about giving money but about human behavior.

> *I was very involved with the youth group between the ages of fifteen and nineteen. People would come in there every Sunday night that, if you said the word* church, *they got nervous. Because of the power we had, we reached out and actually influenced those people to stay away from drugs, to not commit crimes, and all those types of things.*

It seems evident that Cedric believes in the value of the influence of the social group of peers. Youth influence other youth for good or bad concerning a whole range of choices, such as the use of drugs and alcohol, sexual experimentation, and what to wear. Some reciprocity is individual; some is corporate. When youth come together as a group in the context of the church, there is an additional dimension. "Where two or three are gathered in my name . . ." (Matthew 18:20).

Another New Jerseyite described his own experience coming into the youth group. The group influenced Hal's desire to be part of the church and the decisions about where he would give. In addition to his giving decisions being influenced by the church group, he wants his giving to be a positive influence. Hal wants to give

> *. . . where the most people will benefit. I ask myself, "How would I feel about benefiting those people? Are they trying to help themselves or are they people that will abuse? I am inclined to help people who are searching.*

Hal has an interesting standard for where he will direct his giving. For him, a person who is searching is a person who fits the standard. Young adults seemed to be especially concerned that the money they give be used effectively— in whatever way they measure effectiveness. In other words, they want their giving to be a form of positive influence. Many others, especially older people, either trust the institutions or believe that their issue is simply to give. What the recipient does with the money is of no consequence to them, so they claim.

Most givers want their giving to make a difference. By joining together with other Christians, they can see good things happen through their giving. Therefore, most generous givers really want others to join them in the giving journey. More givers mean more money, which means there will be a bigger impact.

In the secular world we read about extremely wealthy people who give away large sums of money and challenge other wealthy people to get involved in philanthropy. Journal articles describe the changing criteria for younger givers. One reason philanthropists give interviews is to influence others to give—and to influence others to consider their criteria for choosing where to give their millions.

Most of the people I interviewed were not among the very wealthy. I doubt that any of the people in this study give away anything close to a hundred thousand dollars in any year, let alone a million or more. We often assume that people who make large contributions ponder long and hard about how to give the money so that it can make the most difference. I discovered that the comparatively small giver also wants the contribution to make a difference.

However, there is also a more personal aspect to the decision to give generously. The decision to give means that the money given is not spent on something else. The givers march to a different drummer and may be unaware that others notice. Although many of them described how others have influenced their giving, few of them see that their giving is an influence on others. For them it is more of a personal spiritual decision, a way to express the connection between the inner witness and the external dimension.

The Congregation as Peer

In the business world, consultants explore the ethos of the work place. The corporate climate at Southwest Airlines is different from the corporate climate at Northwest Airlines. The question is not *whether* corporate climates affect individual actions and attitudes but *how* they affect actions and attitudes. Many questions arise that are beyond the pale of this book. For instance, how was the climate developed in the first place? How is the corporate climate (shared peer influence) communicated in the organization (the church)?

When we look at the influence of a congregation, how does the nature of a congregation affect the giving of the people? How are expectations communicated within the community of faith? Is the act of giving simply between the person and God, or is the congregation's life together part of the motivation to give?

DOES THE CONGREGATION, BY ITS LIFE TOGETHER, TESTIFY THAT GIVING IS IMPORTANT?

Paul wrestled with the power of personal example and group influence when he wrote to the Corinthians about dietary laws (1 Corinthians 8). Eating is a corporate act. Gentiles had no prohibitions against eating certain kinds of meats. Jewish Christians had grown up with the conviction that they should not eat pork, crustaceans, and certain other foods. Paul concluded that there was nothing wrong with eating the forbidden foods, yet, "If food is a cause of their [family members'] falling, I will never eat meat, so that I may not cause one of them to fall" (1 Corinthians 8:13). The power of community customs had to be addressed in the early church.

50

Cultural mores have an enormous impact on our attitudes and actions today.

One young adult from New Jersey acknowledged the power of reciprocity in the group. He acknowledged that most of us are part of many organizations. Each one has expectations. The church is only one of them. Vito named his family and the pressures of being part of the community culture as powerful influences in his life. A former Catholic, he has been a part of a small United Methodist church for only two years.

I have a difficult time saying no. Family and society seems to place more demands on your schedule. Sometimes I spread myself too thin so I don't get the quality out that I could.

It sounds as if he was referring to the quality of his time with his family and the society at large, as well as his relationship to the church where he has become active. Since Vito often spoke of his Catholic background during our conversation, I wondered how much he ascribed his inability to say no to the "brand" of Catholicism of his childhood. He may have been saying that guilt is a strong motivator in him. On the other hand, his generosity may have been the result of compassion, an awakened awareness of the cry for justice from the suffering and the call for mercy from the Almighty.

Hank and Deborah are a young couple with small children. They live in the urban northeastern part of the United States. They described their giving in the face of peer pressure. They remarked that few of their friends ever attend church, and their friends think it is strange that Hank and Deborah have this priority in their life together. Hank said:

When I look around at my friends and at Deborah's friends, I don't see many of them making the same kinds of commitment choices we make. I don't see them giving [time] the same as we give. It is the same way with finances.

Few of the people I interviewed claimed that their generosity was intended to be a witness in the world. Several seemed to recognize that it is a statement of faith, but they do not give in order to make a witness to others. However, generous givers recognize the example of generosity in others as a factor in their own story. They have not made the connection between the peer influence upon their life (which they affirm) and the way their life can be an influence on their peers.

There are dangers when peer influence is used in self-serving ways. There is the potential for great good when a powerful act of witness is used in a healthy way. A Chicago man recognized the dangers of peer pressure. He is an usher and talked about the process of receiving the morning offering in his church. We can detect some uneasiness in his realization that the act of putting (or not putting) money in the plate has peer pressure attached to it.

I take the collection. I always look at the people's hand—if there is something there. There are some people that can't give. It doesn't bother me whether they do or not. I would rather offer them the plate, give them a choice. It doesn't bother me. I hope they realize that.

Even financial secretaries are influenced by the giving of some of the church members. The financial secretary in a California congregation witnessed to the giving she saw from single people in her congregation.

I'm the financial secretary, and I see offerings coming from quite a few single people. And they are single parents, mostly are women. They have to provide for their children. And there is a little lady that just inspires me, because she is over seventy-five, and I say, "How can she do this?" Every month she does this. And on the first Sunday, I know that is a sacrifice for her. There are some of the younger girls who are trying to do that, but it is hard. It is very difficult for them, but they are trying to bring in their offering. Maybe some day they will probably be like this other lady who inspires me. She is just an inspiration to me.

There are at least two ways in which peer group influence was evident in the interviews. One was in the small group, such as a Bible study group or a spiritual support group like the Walk to Emmaus or Covenant Discipleship Groups. The second emerged from people who filled leadership positions in their congregation's capital campaign. In these cases, the campaign leaders met often, prayed together, and worked through their understanding of the congregation's mission. Something happened corporately in that process that rarely happens individually.

Jesus seemed to recognize the power of a positive personal example when he told his followers to "let your light shine before others, so that they may see your good works and give glory to your Father in heaven" (Matthew 5:16). In much the same manner, Paul told the Corinthians, "You yourselves are our letter, written on our hearts, to be known and read by all" (2 Corinthians 3:2). In this era, the life story of Mother Teresa has inspired many people to do good works. The Lay Witness Mission program of The United Methodist Church is based on the conviction that the example of a person's life makes a difference in the beliefs and behaviors of others.[1]

Church leaders have long recognized the value of testimony. Testimony meetings were a staple in the frontier religion in America. During the latter half of the twentieth century, Billy Graham evangelistic crusades enlisted high profile people to testify to their faith during the services. The story of a person's faith journey is considered to be a helpful influence upon others who are somewhere along the road in their spiritual maturation.

I wanted to know if generous givers claimed that they were influenced to give by their peers. While doing background study for this book, I came across a small volume published by The Alban Institute titled *Plain Talk About Churches and Money*. This book describes how three university professors studied giving practices in five diverse denominations in America. They came to the conclusion that peer pressure was one of four major influences on giving. They called it "reciprocity with a social group."[2]

Dean Hoge and his associates pointed out that the primary motivation used by secular fundraisers is reciprocity with someone from the potential giver's social group. In capital funds campaigns, affluent people who make large gifts approach their peers, who also have the resources to give large gifts, and ask them to participate materially in the cause. Similar practices are common in local church capital campaigns. In fact, a major funds campaign in a congregation is rarely successful without "lead gifts" that rely upon this principle. Although the methodology has practical effectiveness, some have questioned the theological merit of using peer group pressure within the church.

The ethical side of the issue is not clear-cut. In 2 Corinthians 8, Paul appealed to the Corinthians to provide an offering to help alleviate the financial problems of the poor in Jerusalem. In his letter, Paul described the generosity of the people in Macedonia. Some readers feel that it was as if he were saying, "They came through with a large offering. I expect you to as well" (see verses 2-4, 7). After highlighting the Macedonians' benevolence, Paul turned to the example of Jesus as a motivation for the Corinthians to give. He said, "You know the generous act of our Lord Jesus Christ, that though he was rich, yet for your sakes he became poor, so that by his poverty you might become rich" (2 Corinthians 8:9).

In that single chapter from the New Testament, Paul seems to link the peer influence of the Macedonian congregation to the influence of God's gift in Jesus Christ. In my experience, local church capital campaigns use peer reciprocity more intentionally than do annual giving campaigns that seek to undergird the ongoing operation of the congregation. The example of Jesus, however, is rarely mentioned in either type of church campaign.

Acts 2 and 3 describe a significant amount of mutual encouragement in the fledgling Christian movement. (There may be a fine line between mutual encouragement and peer pressure.) The "Pentecost people" went so far as holding "all things in common" (see Acts 2:44). As the story of the growing church moves on to chapter 4, we read of a gift made by a follower named Barnabas. He sold a field that he owned and gave the money to the disciples for distribution to those in need (verses 36-37). Immediately after this story is another story of the gift of a land sale. This time the donors were Ananias and Sapphira. They were a married couple who also sold some land and brought proceeds from the sale to the apostles. However, they held back some of the money for their own use—and lied about it to the community of faith (5:1-11).

The juxtaposition of these two stories seems to indicate that Ananias and Sapphira wanted to receive the praise of the early Christian community as they had just witnessed Barnabas receiving. This incident may be the most blatant instance ever recorded of the negative side of peer pressure. A good thing can be twisted and result in bad ends.

The writer of 1 Peter believed in the power of personal example by Christians. He said, "Conduct yourselves honorably among the Gentiles, so that, though they malign you as evildoers, they may see your honorable deeds and glorify God when he comes to judge" (1 Peter 2:12). It seems clear that the Scriptures and church history affirm the power of personal example when used for good. Even the simple (but often difficult) decision to give rather than to buy may be an act of witness in the present age.

Modern Uses of Peer Pressure

I have preached in churches where people who tithe are invited to bring their offerings to the front of the church as a separate ritual from the offerings of the others attending the service. After the tithers have given their offerings, the plates are then passed in the pews so other people may also contribute. There seems to be little doubt that the desire is to encourage people to boost their level of giving to ten percent so that they too can be in "the parade."

Peer influence is sometimes urged but rarely followed in annual giving campaign materials for churches. The materials are likely to be similar to secular fundraising materials, with the addition of "God talk" and worship resources. Materials often emphasize peer group communication. During the days when "every member visitation" was the standard approach (from the 1940's through the 1970's), published programs strongly recommended that large givers go to large givers, medium givers go to medium givers, and those who gave little or nothing were considered leftovers. Regardless of the format for the self-directed campaign materials, almost all of them recommend having personal testimonies told in worship services leading up to commitment Sunday.

Among contemporary local church financial programs, the Quill program makes the most obvious use of peer influence. It is a letter-writing campaign that is built on peer communication. Generous givers write a personal letter to their peers inviting them to join in to "mutually [increase] their giving to the church."[3] The program uses the benefits of peer contact but allows the contact to occur through the "safe" means of a letter rather than through a personal visit.

The Missing Piece: Stewardship for the 1990's, by William M. Easum, also depends heavily on peer communication. It is the method Bill used while he was the pastor of Colonial Hills United Methodist Church in San Antonio, Texas. He invited peer groups to the parsonage and tailored the invitation for them to give in such a way as to communicate most effectively with that particular group.[4] I have to assume that he felt there was great benefit in peers mingling with one another during that evening or afternoon at the parsonage.

Summary

We come back now to the two questions asked at the beginning of this chapter: (1) Are generous givers, in fact, influenced by peers to give generously? and (2) Is it appropriate for church leaders to use peer influence to encourage greater generosity? In other words, can peer influence be used without becoming manipulative?

The answer to the first question seems obvious: People *are* influenced by their peers. The entire purpose of advertising is influence. However, influence is heavily dependent upon modeling, training, and earlier life experiences.

Peer influence can be either positive or negative. The church's task is to develop a supportive fellowship rooted in biblical values that will counter unhealthy peer influence from the world around us. People often come into the life of a church seeking that kind of direction and support.

As for the second question, the use of peer influence in the church is complicated. There will be peer influence in a church—for good or for ill. Church leaders need to exercise vigilance so that the church does not become seduced by the values that are counter to the faith. The question is, What kind of influence will we encourage? Christians are called upon to be stewards of the influence they have both inside the church and in the larger community. What are the expectations that are communicated? Do we convey high expectations or low expectations to the congregation? People tend to live up or down to the expectations of their peer group.

Peer influence is a fact of life. When the peer influence is shaped and directed by the Spirit of God within the community of faith, there is the potential for this energy to be used for good. Vigilance is crucial so that the power is not used in manipulative ways.

Endnotes

1 See www.gbod.org/evangelism/programs/laywitness for more information.

2 Reprinted from *Plain Talk About Churches and Money*, by Dean Hoge, Patrick McNamara, and Charles Zech, by permission of the Alban Institute, Inc., 7315 Wisconsin Avenue, Suite 1250W, Bethesda, Maryland 20814-3211. Copyright © 1997. All rights reserved; page 39. According to *Money Matters: Personal Giving in American Churches* (Westminster John Knox Press, 1996), the five denominations studied were The Assemblies of God, The Southern Baptist Convention, The Roman Catholic Church, The Evangelical Lutheran Church in America, and The Presbyterian Church (U.S.A.).

3 See *How to Increase Giving in Your Church: An Introduction to Quill*, by Gary Arnold (Quill, Inc., 1995). Quotation from *Quill: The Personal Witness Stewardship Program, Fund-Raising Council Member Manual*, by Gary Arnold (Quill, Inc., 1995); page 6.

4 See *The Missing Piece: Stewardship for the 1990's*, by William M. Easum (21st Century Strategies, Inc., 1990).

To Put This Chapter Into Practice

Individuals

1. Name the people who have influenced your attitudes toward giving—positively and negatively.
2. List the groups you have been a part of during your life. Which groups had a positive influence? Which had a negative influence? Which ones affected your current practice of giving?
3. Who are the people who may be influenced by you? How will you invest that influence? Are there changes you need to make so that the influence can be more positive?

Church Leaders

1. Train people to lead *Disciple* Bible study. Start with the thirty-four-week basic study, *Disciple: Becoming Disciples Through Bible Study* (The United Methodist Publishing House). Take the course yourself, and encourage others in the church to enroll.
2. Encourage people from your church and community to go on a Walk to Emmaus weekend retreat.
3. Invite people in the congregation to describe their own spiritual pilgrimage in giving. They may tell their stories in a worship service and/or in Sunday school classes.
4. Examine letters and church newsletter articles that were sent to the congregation during the past years. What expectations were communicated? What changes will you make in order to communicate healthier expectations in the year ahead?
5. Spend ten minutes at the beginning of a Board/Council meeting to pair up and let each person tell the story of his or her first recollection of church giving.

4

Does Giving Help a Person Be All She or He Can Be?

. . . from an economic rationality point of view, giving money away is irrational, because then the actor has less left for himself or herself. This is true. But we need to know who "himself" or "herself" refers to. It may sound simple, but in reality it is not.[1]

The authors of *Plain Talk About Churches and Money* pose an interesting quandary. Is giving an irrational act? In fact, are any of our money decisions the result of rational deliberation? Do we spend and give through reasoned calculation or to meet inner needs, or does giving flow from some other root?

Hoge and his associates illustrated their point about the relationship between self-interest and giving with the example of kidney donors. They pointed out that most kidney donors are members of the recipient's family. Family members are apparently more willing to contribute a kidney than a casual acquaintance is. The closer the relationship, the more likely the person is to give. The gift is an extension of the self. In giving the kidney, the person becomes more human, more loving.[2] Love is more than a feeling; action puts feet to the love. Sharing financial resources is another kind of action.

Fulfillment in life emerges within community. As I listened to generous people tell their stories, I heard people relate their giving to the affirmation that they are all part of a larger family. A portion of the conversion experience is the affirmation that we are part of God's family. The story in Acts 10 illustrates the changing understanding of kinship within God's family. Peter dreamed about a sheet that was lowered from heaven and contained all sorts of foods that were forbidden by Hebrew law. Only after he received the message that God had made all food and it was all good, did Peter recognize that a Roman was part of God's family. He was then free to go to the centurion and participate in his life. The family circle was redrawn and it became inclusive. Those who were seen as far off were now brought near through the good news of Jesus Christ.

HOW BIG IS YOUR CIRCLE OF INCLUSION? DOES IT INCLUDE THE WHOLE COMMUNITY? DOES IT INCLUDE THE WHOLE WORLD?

Many people wrestle with how they fit into the bigger picture of life. How big is the circle of inclusion? How do I know who I am? It is not surprising that the act of giving is a significant part of many people's process of discovering who they are and asserting their own identity. For some, giving begins at a young age. A grandmother told a story of her granddaughter who was five years old:

> *She fills out an envelope when she goes to church. One time she was writing on her envelope. She put twenty-five cents in it. She marched right up to the front and gave the envelope to the pastor. She wanted to be part of this.*

Seeing the church as an extension of one's family is common among all ages, but it is often expressed in different manners. Younger people seem to relate giving to the local congregation or even to a particular group within the congregation more than to any explicit understanding of the church's wider mission. I remember a young man saying years ago, "This [Sunday school] class is my church." It was where he fit in.

Most of the people I interviewed named their identity within the local congregation instead of describing themselves as part of God's grand scheme of things for the whole world. Although these attitudes were widespread among the young adults, the same way of thinking is not uncommon among older people. A grandparent in Texas said:

> *Our church is part of our family. We are heavily involved. Probably our minds revolve around our church activity.*

A young man talked enthusiastically about being a part of a developing congregation in a booming suburban area of Dallas, Texas. Stefan identified the mission of the church as reaching out to the new residents streaming into the community. If he saw the mission as something beyond the immediate community, it was not evident in his remarks.

We are building the ability to reach out to others. We really feel like we are part of something.

However, we cannot draw the conclusion that the circle is limited on the basis of brief remarks by a person enthusiastic about the present opportunity. It is doubtful that a church can do very much reaching out unless it has a base from which to operate. The self-identity of the local congregation as a community/family is a vital foundation for reaching beyond itself. It is unlikely that one's primary identity can be formed beyond the community. A congregation has little self-identity unless there is a feeling among the people that they are connected to one another.

The connectedness often has special value for racial-ethnic groups. For instance, a Hispanic layperson in California described the coming of age of his congregation. They had been a mission church during their formative years. Most of the funds came from external agencies. He said:

When my generation was growing up and getting married, learning the ins and outs of the church, we no longer wanted to ask for help [from the denomination]. We should do it ourselves. That is what helped us focus on being a self-sufficient church, to be faithful in our giving—and we set tithing as our goal. We can't withhold anything from God.

Investing the Self

Most generous givers do not describe "going to church." They believe they are an integral part of the church. It is part of their identity. It is who they are. They not only *do* it; they *are* it. They experience a unique relationship with Christ and with the people of the congregation. The connection between identity, caring, and giving was beautifully expressed by a young woman from a suburban Dallas congregation when she said:

We are contributing to an experience of the rest of our lives—a congregation who cares.

A major question is, How large is the caring circle of your church? Several people who told their stories see their giving as part of something much bigger than the membership of their congregation. They are not what God intended them to be unless they participate in this larger family of all God's people. Josh, a retired CPA, described it in these words:

Last Sunday we had a collection of food to help people who needed food. To me that is sort of like that newspaper article that listed all [that our church] did. Maybe that's the warm fuzzy feeling you get. I didn't run out and deliver a bag of groceries to the family that lost everything in the fire. But I feel part of it, for you make a contribution to the church. By association, I am part of the total.

The church where I worship includes people from approximately thirty different nations of birth. I have had very little to do with reaching out to these people from the Pacific Islands, Africa, Europe, Asia, the Philippines, and other parts of the world. Although I know several of the international people and have formed friendships with some, I have not served on the Multicultural Committee at the church. Yet I take pride in the reality that our church is a virtual mini-United Nations.

Patricia, a middle-aged woman in a Virginia church, described her joy at work projects engaged in by others from her church. I could sense her satisfaction and sense of participation when she enthusiastically told about the involvement:

Some people from the congregation have gone on a VIM [Volunteers In Mission] project in Haiti. A group from here went to help in the flood relief in Missouri.

We are part of something bigger than ourselves when we become a part of a congregation. The act of relating to a church is a statement that one's world is bigger than oneself. Giving is a symbol of seeing ourselves in relationship with God and with God's creation. We are identified as being part of God's new people (see 1 Peter 2:9). A young adult in western Virginia expressed a similar attitude:

I feel that our church has a lot of good programs and does a lot of good work in a lot of fields. Obviously, you feel a sense of pride. You get a feeling of satisfaction when you sense the money is going for some good causes and good things. And I feel good that we are doing a decent part of that. When you are a part of that, you do sense pride; there is a certain sense of worth that it is going for a good cause.

As I heard these words, my mind went to the crowd at an athletic contest. At the end of the game it is not unusual for people pouring out of the stands to say to one another, "Hurrah! We won!" or, "Darn. We lost." They did not play one second in the game, but they felt part of the game anyway.

The act of contributing to the ministries of the church represents the relationship of the giver to God and to the community of faith. Martín, an active church member from Ventura, California, addressed this concept:

Because my money to me manifests my time, manifests my life, I am giving part of myself. At that moment [during the offering], I am sharing with others.

Perhaps Martín nailed the real central issue. Authentic giving is the giving of oneself. In authentic giving, the person gives himself or herself with the gift. The poor who give may have a clearer sense that they are giving of themselves. If you have much of this world's goods, a gift may be a transaction. If you have little and share the little you have, a gift often touches the core of one's life. It is a giving of oneself. In that sense, giving is deep sharing more than it is an offering.

> I would say [giving] is a very practical necessity for perpetuating the church. But I think there is a deeper significance also. What we are really doing here is building. That giving is a way of helping us perpetuate our reaching out, and the giving part of it enables us to give back. I want to give back.

People do not feel complete when they are cut off from one another. Unless a person sees himself or herself as bigger than one's self, there is no healthy identity. Giving provides both the opportunity and the vehicle for people to become a part of something bigger.

Identity and Direction

Part of the decision about where a person will channel his or her giving is related to the individual's sense of feeling a part of the church. In the book *Revolutionizing Christian Stewardship for the 21st Century*, Dan Dick described church participation in terms of a cosmology. He identified the relationship to the congregation in terms of the Solar Center, Inner Planets, the Asteroid Belt, Outer Planets, and Lost in Space. Those in the Solar Center are the people who give of their time, energy, and money. As we follow the cosmology from the center outward, the people's identity with the congregation and their contributions of both time and money diminish.[3]

People in the solar center are not only likely to channel their giving through the church but also more likely to be generous givers to all causes. Secular nonprofit organizations develop profiles of prospective givers. They know that any person who is active in a local church is more likely to give than a person who does not regularly participate in the life of a congregation.

The bottom line is that acquiring more and more does not bring satisfaction to life. Many expensive "toys" often make a person less sure of who he or she is. Accumulation of lots of stuff may only bring confusion about what is at the center. Not being able to afford decent housing or not having enough food does not make a person happy either. Jesus did not romanticize poverty even though he constantly warned of the dangers of becoming distracted from the abundant life by the abundance of things.

People who give do receive a payback. Most generous givers have a sense that what they are doing is important. Their giving is important to their own soul, and it makes a difference in the world. Givers are affirmed when the church communicates how their giving is making a difference in the lives of folks around the world. The givers appreciate that feedback.

In many business books since W. Edwards Deming burst onto the American manufacturing scene, much has been written about making customers happy. The giver is not a customer in the same sense as a person wandering through a department store; however, there are some interesting analogies. Customers may not always know exactly what they are looking for. When their need is matched with the store's product, everyone is happy.

The clerk receives satisfaction when he or she is able to link the customer with the item on the rack. In a similar way, I enjoy helping people who call or e-mail my office. I find great personal satisfaction in helping people accomplish what they want to accomplish. In some cases, they simply want to know where to get a resource. In other cases, they may want a listening ear when they describe a dilemma. Usually they can figure out the solution for themselves. Part of my identity is my ability to listen and to respond when appropriate.

My wife is a real estate agent. She gets satisfaction in helping people find the home they are looking for. Sure, she wants to make the customer happy, but it isn't pure and simple altruism. When she has done her job well, she has satisfaction that she is a good professional. The feedback of the people provides encouragement to her. In a similar way, when generous givers write checks to the church or sign the bank authorization for contributions through electronic funds transfer, they need feedback in order to recognize that what they are doing is important. Generous givers need reinforcement. Feedback helps authenticate their participation in ministry in the name of Jesus Christ.

WHAT KIND OF FEEDBACK DO YOU GIVE THE GIVERS IN YOUR CONGREGATION?

People move from strength to strength, not from weakness to strength. The task of leadership is to notice where people's strengths are and to affirm those strengths. Then the people can explore ways to make their strengths and gifts more helpful in the world.

Discovering who we are is not a one-time task. Conversion is the door to growth in the Spirit, not the end of growth. Developing one's spiritual life is not like building a Ford Taurus or a Dell computer. We do not roll off an assembly line and work until we finally die. Instead, the life of faith is more like a marriage. Spouses need to renegotiate their relationship about every eight to ten years. Saying "I do" is not the end of the task. It is the beginning.

In the same way, we do not settle our giving once and for all as part of our whole faith journey. That is why churches have annual giving campaigns. (At least, it should be one of the reasons.) The purpose of a campaign is not simply to underwrite the budget but to help people explore whether their giving is keeping up to where they are journeying in their faith. Is giving helping the giver be all that he or she can be?

Biblical Reflection

A Christian does not see different things from what other people see. A Christian does, however, see the same things through a different lens. Generous givers are not blind to material things. They see money and possessions, but they see them as something to share. They look upon giving as a privilege rather than as a duty. They struggle with money decisions, but they have a different basis for making the determination about what to do. There are many biblical models.

Most of the prophetic books of the Old Testament were written to the people living in exile in Babylon. They had been forcibly removed from their homeland and taken to a strange land. They were cut off from the Temple. The Jerusalem Temple symbolized their identity around the God they called Yahweh. Now, in this strange land with no Temple, they were not sure who they were. They were in despair.

Many people today feel cut off from the dependable traditions of a previous time. They too are not sure who they are or what their future is. When there is no centering identity, many people in affluent North America attempt to fill their lives with things. In contrast, generous givers find an identity that they can name. The church's task is to help people find their identity in Jesus Christ. Then, and only then, can the people find and express their identity as the people of God through their words and their actions. One of those actions is to share the resources they have to manage.

The letter of 1 Peter was written "to the exiles" (1 Peter 1:1). The writer affirmed the identity of these cut-off people. In and through the gift of Jesus' resurrection they were not, in fact, cut off (verse 3). They were told that they had been blessed. That is not the end of the story. Blessing carries a responsibility. If we don't know who (and whose) we are, we can hardly be responsible.

This concept is reflected beautifully in this traditional communion prayer that incorporates language from 1 Peter: "Here we offer ourselves in obedience to you, through the perfect offering of your Son, Jesus Christ, giving you thanks that you have called us to be a royal priesthood, a holy nation, your own people; and to you, O God, Creator, Redeemer, and Sanctifier, be ascribed blessing and honor and glory and power for ever and ever. Amen."[4]

Endnotes

1 Reprinted from *Plain Talk About Churches and Money*, by Dean Hoge, Patrick McNamara, and Charles Zech, by permission of the Alban Institute, Inc., 7315 Wisconsin Avenue, Suite 1250W, Bethesda, Maryland 20814-3211. Copyright © 1997. All rights reserved; page 44.

2 See *Plain Talk About Churches and Money*, by Dean Hoge, Patrick McNamara, and Charles Zech (The Alban Institute, 1997); pages 45–46.

3 See *Revolutionizing Christian Stewardship for the 21st Century: Lessons From Copernicus*, by Dan R. Dick (Discipleship Resources, 1997); pages 72–86.

4 As printed in *The New Interpreter's Bible*, Volume XII (Abingdon Press, 1998); page 269.

To Put This Chapter Into Practice

Individuals

1. Write down five experiences, events, or actions in your life that brought you real happiness. How did those experiences shape the way you understand yourself? Did money have anything to do with them? If so, in what way?
2. Read the words of the hymn "Blessed Assurance" (*The United Methodist Hymnal*, 369). Can you sing it with any confidence?
3. When you place your money in the offering plate next Sunday (or write the next check to the church), meditate on ways you are giving of yourself to the world, to the community, to the church, and to God.

Finance Committees

1. Write an article for the church newspaper that describes giving as investing in God's ministry to others.
2. At the time the offering is received in your worship service, tell a story about the way the money helps others.
3. Work with other leaders in the congregation to help all of the members and constituents grow in their relationship with Jesus Christ. Help them identify themselves as God's people and as parts of both the local congregation and the denomination.

5

Does God Reward Generosity?

⌒

Is God really open to building up reciprocal relationships? Is God mindful of gifts from individuals, and will God make an effort to repay them later?[1]

What is the definition of *generosity*? I asked church leaders to arrange interviews with generous givers, but I did not define *generosity* except with the following comment: "As you select the people, remember that the most generous person I can think of in the Bible is a woman who put two small coins in a Temple offering box." The selectors seemed to do an excellent job of choosing a wide variety of generous givers for my interviews.

The Oxford Universal Dictionary provides two definitions of *generosity* that have nothing to do with money or giving before they get to definition number 3, "Liberality in giving, munificence."[2] I suspect that most church leaders think of financial generosity when they hear the word, regardless of the order of the dictionary definitions. When I illustrated generosity by referring to the biblical story of a woman who placed two small coins in the Temple offering box, I probably skewed the consideration directly to financial giving even if the person would not normally think in those terms.

The most important factor in any kind of generosity is not the amount given but the heart of the giver. That is true of both money and time.

However, the most usual indicator of generosity is the proportion of the person's financial resources given out of what he or she has to give.

The most common understanding of generosity in the church is large proportionate giving. That is not to deny that there are many nonfinancial forms of generosity. Nearly every person interviewed understood giving in financial terms. Many of them connected the financial giving to other kinds of giving.

With that understanding of generosity, the question remains: Does God reward those who are generous? If generosity is rewarded, what is the nature of the reward? These questions have bothered Christian people down through the centuries. They bother this writer. Jesus denounced selfishness, yet he often spoke about rewards. He seemed to vigorously condemn systems and people that put others into poverty, but he did not promise his followers earthly riches. Sharing of one's resources is affirmed over and over again in the Scriptures of both the Old and New Testaments. Sometimes the command to share is accompanied by a promise of a reward; many times no such promise is included.

I can find no example of quid pro quo in the Bible indicating that people will gather in more and more money if they give more to the religious institution or some other charitable purpose. Stories of saints who lived in poverty are recorded throughout human history. Most of the people I greatly admire are not people who became rich. If ever a relationship was shrouded in mystery, the relationship between giving and rewards seems to be a prime example.

The relationship between generosity and reward is a pragmatic matter for some people in the church. Greed can become a motivation for giving if the person believes that God will make anyone rich who gives generously. Indeed, some of the people who talked with me claimed that God blessed them when they started giving more generously. At first I thought they were saying that giving generously made them

AS FOR THOSE WHO IN THE PRESENT AGE ARE RICH, COMMAND THEM NOT TO BE HAUGHTY, OR TO SET THEIR HOPES ON THE UNCERTAINTY OF RICHES, BUT RATHER ON GOD WHO RICHLY PROVIDES US WITH EVERYTHING FOR OUR ENJOYMENT. THEY ARE TO DO GOOD, TO BE RICH IN GOOD WORKS, GENEROUS, AND READY TO SHARE, THUS STORING UP FOR THEMSELVES THE TREASURE OF A GOOD FOUNDATION FOR THE FUTURE, SO THAT THEY MAY TAKE HOLD OF THE LIFE THAT REALLY IS LIFE.

(1 TIMOTHY 6:17-19)

more affluent. Then I listened more carefully. That did not seem to be the point they were trying to communicate. For instance, Mrs. Henry, a woman from Los Angeles said:

I have come up with this feeling—the more you give away, the more God blesses you.

Two important questions are raised by Mrs. Henry's comment. First, what did she mean by *blesses?* North Americans seem to naturally assume that all blessings are financial or material. But are increased financial resources necessarily the only way to define a blessing? Some anecdotal evidence suggests that those with the most money in the present era are some of the most miserable people in the world. The more stuff we have, the more likely we are to build walls around our property and spend large amounts of money for alarm systems to protect it. Possessions have a way of possessing the person.

If we assume that Mrs. Henry meant that she had more money coming in when she gave more generously, we may be imputing our cultural presupposition to her comment rather than hearing her meaning. Mrs. Henry used the phrase, "I have come up with this feeling . . ." Her statement was a reflection on her experience rather than a calculation of a strategy. She is trying to make sense of the experiences in her life. She gave generously; she felt blessed. Her rationale came after the fact rather than prior to the decision to give more generously.

Another Californian talked about the relationship of rewards to her giving. Helen described receiving after she gave, but she distinctly defined the reward in noneconomic terms when she said:

I felt like the more I gave out towards the church, the more I got back in rewards of comfort and love and understanding.

The rewards she named were not money or possessions but comfort, love, and understanding. No monetary value can be put on these qualities. Although few were as explicit as Helen in describing God's reciprocity, her words seemed to be implied in many of the stories told by others.

Koreans and Blessings

Korean participants in this project consistently raised the issue of rewards. For many of them, the material blessings seemed to be intertwined with spiritual blessings. Susie, a young Korean woman from California, said:

I gave ten percent out of my paycheck. I want to tell you—when I did that, He gave me blessings. I give and He gives me more than what I have given to Him. And then when time goes on, it becomes mandatory. I give because I have to—inside. I tell God, "Bless me more so I can help others."

Notice the interweaving of feelings, attitudes, and monetary return. There is inner compulsion and external confirmation. At first I thought Susie claimed that her generous giving was to make her wealthier. Then, at the end of her response to my question, she identified the purpose of the greater amount of money she received. It was to help others. The more she got, the more she had to give away. What an unusual reward system!

Where Does It Begin?

For some people, reciprocity with God seemed to be a clear-cut contractual obligation with a defined division of labor. You have your responsibility; God has God's responsibility. They are separate but dependent upon each other. A Texas grandmother described a clearly defined three-pocket theory:

You pay your God. That is your commitment. You pay yourself. That's your savings. You live on what's left. If you do that, you will never run out of money.

In this kind of formulation, there is give and take but the person is the originator and God responds. Many of the people who spoke of reciprocity operated out of an understanding that they initiated the actions. Such a formulation throws us into a theological debate that has gone on for generations. On one side of the argument, the human is powerless to do anything. Everything is up to God. The human task is to respond to what God initiates. Even the human response is possible only by the grace of God. The opposite end of the spectrum believes that almost everything is up to human decision and action. In this understanding, God is fairly passive and may or may not respond to human actions. For some, God's response is active. In fact, God seems duty bound to act in response. For others, the response is simply the unfolding of previously set "laws" of reciprocity. Heidi Sanders may have expressed the contractual obligation when she said:

The blessings do come when you give back to God. My minister brother taught me this.

Heidi's comments do not make it clear whether humans are the prime initiator or God is the prime initiator. By using the term "give back," she implies that God is the initiator. However, some people use that term as a casual expression, virtually empty of meaning. I could not tell whether she simply mouthed a phrase or if she had thought through what it means for God to give back in response to our giving back. It seems quite clear that a number of givers expect God to respond with a blessing when they "give back."

Many of the generous people in this study had this sense of responsibility. They had an inner compulsion to "give back"—not in the sense of paying God back for some specific good but in the sense of responding in a tangible, human way to blessings that have come and will come from

God. They are under obligation to pass blessings on to others. Some do this through generous giving. Their motivation seems to echo the psalmist who asked,

> What shall I return to the LORD
> for all his bounty to me?
> (Psalm 116:12)

Tom Novak from Rhode Island made a Christian commitment in his middle adult years. For most of his life he had intellectual problems with Christian theology. A relative suggested that he read some of the works of the Catholic theologian Matthew Fox. Tom found a soul mate. Fox's writings made it possible for him to say yes to the faith and join the church. Now he writes a monthly column in the church newsletter. In talking about a recent column, Tom said:

> *When you give more, you get more from it. You have a sacred feeling when you do the giving. That is one of the ways God speaks to us. It is the big "I," God, giving through the little "I," us.*

God is the initiator in Tom's understanding. The giver is a channel of God's giving to the world rather than being an initiator, a bystander, or an observer. To be a channel of God's love is to be a blessing. People who are channels of God's blessing do not denigrate their own participation, nor do they claim more than their due.

Thanksgiving

People can respond to God's grace in many ways. By definition, grace is a gift. It is not deserved but freely given. Thanksgiving is one of the most common emotions to an undeserved gift. Thanksgiving is a human way of affirming a relationship.

In the opening of Paul's tender letter to the beloved Philippians, he says: "I thank my God every time I remember you" (Philippians 1:3). Near the end of that brief letter, Paul acknowledges a monetary gift that was sent via Epaphroditus (4:10-20). Paul received the monetary gift from the Philippian church as a sign of their affection. He had not asked them for any money, but he deeply appreciated their support. Paul's letter was an acknowledgement and affirmation of the relationship.

Many of the people in this study described how God initiated the relationship with them. Their generous giving was viewed as a response to God's initiative rather than an insurance program to establish a relationship with God. Instead of purchasing a blessing, they were responding to blessings. The word *blessing* describes a gift received rather than a calculated action on the part of the one on the receiving end.

One day I sat in a restaurant with a staff person from another denomina-tional agency. Eugene is Korean. I said to him, "Most Korean Christians seem to see tithing as automatic. They rarely question the practice. Help me to understand what is different about Koreans and Euro-Americans. Does Korean culture have a dimension that makes tithing natural? Does the acceptance of tithing have something to do with the way the Christian faith was presented in the first place? To what do you ascribe the Korean Chris-tian's enthusiasm for tithing?" Eugene immediately responded, "Many Koreans are first-generation Christians. We remember what it was like when we were not Christians. We are grateful."

I heard a kindred story of God's intervention from a man in Dallas, Texas. God brought hope out of despair and life out of death for him. Alfred responded to my question about the roots of his giving with the following:

> *Experience! I am a recovering alcoholic. During those times I wasn't thinking about giving. I was thinking about taking. That was my lifestyle. That was then. Now is now. When I came to Jubilee, what got it all started was* Disciple 1. *That is what started it. Giving is part of my worship to God. I had never picked up the Bible. In* Disciple *we had to study. I got to reading the Word. I got hungry for the Word. I got to see how powerful it was.*

It seemed clear that Alfred saw giving as a symbol of the new life he had in Christ and the church. Giving was a way he could respond out of the joy he experienced in his new life. He gave out of a thankful heart. It was a means to continue a relationship that was very dear to him.

People who experienced poverty during an earlier time in their life some-times give in gratitude for their new economic stability. It is clear that getting out of poverty is seen as a blessing for those who have experienced it. Coleen raised four children on welfare. Now Coleen has a decent job. She is able to pay her bills. Now she can financially contribute to her church. She described the root of her thankfulness.

> *My attitude is that I've been blessed so abundantly, and I just look forward to giving.*

Coleen made a connection between material stuff and God's blessing. But the relationship was described not with a sense of greed but with a sense of gratitude. Many people would feel very poor if they had no more of this world's goods than Coleen, yet anecdotal evidence suggests that poor peo-ple are often more willing to ascribe any good fortune that comes to them as a gift from God. Affluent people are more apt to think that their good fortune is through their own wisdom or cunning. Some people vividly remember when things were worse. They are thankful for the change in economic status in their lives.

Not all thankful people had such a dramatic turnaround as Alfred. Not all of them were once on welfare like Coleen. Not all generous givers have known the realities of hunger. However, it may be that those who never suffered deprivation find it more difficult to recognize the ways they have been blessed.

Bonnie is the parent of a five-year-old and a ten-year-old. I do not know about Bonnie's financial condition or whether she would fall in the lower, middle, or upper class economically. There is no doubt that Bonnie is surprised by her present economic condition. She expressed her thankfulness (gratitude) in these words when asked to describe her giving:

> . . . the fact that where I am today, I feel blessed. I feel like I have an abundance of many things.

A person's attitude about abundance or scarcity has more to do with the person's perspective on life than it does on his or her bank account or material things accumulated. Some people count friends. Others count health. Still others may be grateful for family or for the era in which they live. Yet, the economic dimension of life is so dominant in North American culture that it is not surprising that many people describe their blessings in economic terms.

It is out of that understanding of a blessing that many of the interviewees named their *obligation* to give back. The terms they used echoed the conclusion of Jesus' parable of the faithful and unfaithful slaves:

> From everyone to whom much has been given, much will be required;
> and from the one to whom much has been entrusted, even more will
> be demanded. (Luke 12:48)

Jesus drew a moral from the tale of the slaves who tried to see what they could get away with in contrast with those who were faithful. Many of the generous givers I interviewed believed that they had been given much and were inwardly required to respond to their abundance.

Gratitude as a Motivation

Researchers search for the motivation for giving. I am convinced that most of the research is flawed because it looks for one motivation. God's human creatures are much more complex than that. Most of us have layer upon layer of motivation. In some circumstances we may operate out of one motivation. In other circumstances we may respond in a different manner. In all probability, two or three (or more) different motivational forces are working within us whenever we make a decision about what to do with money we control.

Some researchers provide a list of possible motivations and ask the respondents to rate the list from highest to lowest. When people are given such a list, they will almost always select gratitude as their number one motivation. However, when people are asked open-ended questions about the motivation for their giving, gratitude is likely to be second or even lower on the list of answers.

COUNT YOUR BLESSINGS,

NAME THEM ONE BY ONE; . . .

COUNT YOUR MANY BLESSINGS,

SEE WHAT GOD HATH DONE.

(JOHNSON OATMAN, JR.)

Gratitude is an internal motivation that is expressed in different ways by different people. Some people rarely consider that they have anything to be grateful for. They think only of what they feel they deserve. I found a general difference in gratitude among different generations. The generality is that young adults are more sensitive to gratitude as one of the motivating factors underneath their giving than are Baby Boomers.

A young adult from Nashville, Tennessee, said that she felt so fortunate that she felt an obligation to give. In a 1990 focus group with Houston, Texas, Baby Boomers I discovered that the word *obligation* drew a negative, even hostile, reaction. Boomers see it as something imposed upon them from outside. Among Generation X adults, I found no such aversion. *Obligation* is not a bad word for them. Instead, it is an inner push that helps them act in a way that fulfills who they are trying to become.

The Power of Feedback

Money was not an issue in some of my conversations about reciprocity. A young couple from New Jersey invested a lot of time working with the youth program at their church. They would have loved to get more feedback, but they recognized that teenagers seldom bother to thank the adults who work with them for the time and energy invested in them. They believed they had come to terms with that reality. A telling remark was:

> *How does it feel when you don't think you will get anything in return? Sometimes it feels really good. Sometimes I don't think about it at all. There are times when you are giving and getting criticism about it—fifth- and sixthhand—something that happened—by people who are not doing anything at all. It is a little frustrating.*

Positive feedback is important to most givers. That does not mean that they want a public commendation or a plaque hung in the church to proclaim their generosity. It means that they deeply appreciate hearing that their giving is making a difference in the world. That kind of information is positive feedback. In the case of the young couple from New Jersey, they were able to trust that the feedback would eventually come although they had not yet received it. Confidence in delayed gratification may be important to givers.

Further Biblical Reflections

Many of the people who talked to me about their giving believed that the reciprocal blessing was emphatically not financial. Others expressed attitudes and opinions suggesting their conviction that there is a financial quid pro quo.

"CHURCHES THAT EMPHASIZE GIVING TO GOD RECEIVE LOWER PER MEMBER CONTRIBUTIONS THAN DO THOSE CHURCHES CONVEYING A DIFFERENT MESSAGE."[3]

The different perspectives among generous Christian givers have their roots in ancient stories of faith. Many passages in the Hebrew Bible struggle with the relationship of prosperity to faithfulness. God promised Abraham that he would be a great nation (Genesis 12:2). His great flocks and herds are clearly described as part of the blessing that came to this family that left their homeland in Haran and ventured by faith into the land of promise.

In a variety of places throughout the Hebrew Scriptures, blessing seems to be associated with great property holdings and magnificent buildings. This philosophy is common in the Book of Proverbs. The writer boldly states:

> A generous person will be enriched, . . .
> The people curse those who hold back grain,
>   but a blessing is on the head of those who sell it.
>   (Proverbs 11:25a, 26)

Monetary blessing is also affirmed by the statement that "prosperity rewards the righteous" (Proverbs 13:21). The following verse carries the same theme when it claims that

> The good leave an inheritance to their children's children,
>   but the sinner's wealth is laid up for the righteous.
>   (Proverbs 13:22)

We read these biblical words with our North American individualistic eyes. Our Hebrew ancestors were much more likely to think in terms of the tribe and nation rather than the individual. In addition, we read with our modern expectation of instant results. We are dumbfounded by the four hundred years between the time when the Israelites were first enslaved in Egypt and the time when Moses was finally sent to bring them out. We can hardly imagine forty years of wandering in the wilderness.

In both ways of reading and interpreting the Proverbs 13:22 passage, we may be distorting its meaning. Some commentators believe that the biblical promise is an affirmation that justice will finally be restored in the land. It may or may not bring riches to the individual. Abraham was a symbol of a nation as much as he was an individual person.

In contrast with the ascription of righteousness with wealth that we find in portions of the Scriptures, the Apocryphal book Wisdom of Solomon is forthright about the reward of the righteous. It states

> But the righteous live for ever,
> and their reward is with the Lord.
> (Wisdom of Solomon 5:15)

The Hebrew people believed that God was Lord of all. Our compartmentalizing of the sacred and the secular would make no sense to the Hebrew people. If we claim that God does not care about our economic condition, we have limited God. God is either the God of the entirety or the God of nothing. To the Hebrews, the extraordinary God was God of the ordinary. Nothing, no matter how mundane, was outside the scope of God's concern. If we deny that God has anything to do with the prosperity of a person or of a nation, we have barred recognition of God's action in an important sphere of life.

Leviticus 26 is explicit about the blessings that come through obedience to God's rules. The chapter starts out with an admonition to "make for yourselves no idols" and to "keep my sabbaths" (verses 1 and 2). Both exhortations come directly from the Ten Commandments. Then, in verses 3 through 13, we find a series of promises. The promises are so grand that they almost sound like a return to the garden of Eden. They include abundant crops, peace, and large, healthy families.

IF YOU THINK YOU HAVE IT MADE BECAUSE YOU LIVE IN A FANCY HOUSE AND GO TO THE MOST EXPENSIVE RESTAURANTS IN TOWN, WATCH OUT! YOU MAY HAVE SEASON TICKETS TO THE SYMPHONY AND OTHER CULTURAL EVENTS. YOU MAY BUY ANY CD YOU WANT. FREQUENT VISITS TO THE BEAUTY SALON AND THE ATHLETIC CLUB MAY BE PART OF YOUR LIFE, BUT BEWARE IF YOU ARE NOT DEEPLY TROUBLED BY THE PROBLEMS OF THE POOR. YOU CAN DO SOMETHING ABOUT IT! (AMOS 6:4-6, PARAPHRASED)

Immediately following the promises, beginning with verse 14, the lawgiver identifies a long list of penalties upon the nation if the commandments are not kept. The people will not be able to eat the crops they plant, their nation will be overrun with enemies, disease and death will plague their families, and the place of worship will be in ruins. Utter chaos will reign in the land. It is a description of Eden before God brought order to the chaos.

Prosperity for God's faithful is not a contractual obligation upon the Almighty. Prophets poured out their condemnation of those who became prosperous while flaunting their own righteousness. Amos, the shepherd of Tekoa, left no doubt about his denunciation of those who prospered while neglecting the needs of the downtrodden.

> Alas for those who lie on beds of ivory,
> and lounge on their couches,
> and eat lambs from the flock,
> and calves from the stall;
> who sing idle songs to the sound of the harp,
> and like David improvise on instruments of music;
> who drink wine from bowls,
> and anoint themselves with the finest oils,
> but are not grieved over the ruin of Joseph!
> (Amos 6:4-6)

Many of the words of Jesus echoed the proclamations of the prophets. When he addressed the issue of public prayer, he described two different kinds of rewards. If your prayer is for show, you will receive the acclaim of folks. If your prayer is for a personal relationship with God, your reward will be in that relationship. What you desire is what you get. But what you get may not be what is best for you. I once heard a pastor say something akin to, "Hell is when you get what you wanted but it isn't what you should have had."

If treasure is what our heart desires, we will focus on the kind of treasure we desire. It seems clear from the Gospel records that Jesus did not want his followers to seek after riches. In a well-known saying, Jesus directed his followers:

> Do not be afraid, little flock, for it is your Father's good pleasure to give you the kingdom. Sell your possessions, and give alms. Make purses for yourselves that do not wear out, an unfailing treasure in heaven, where no thief comes near and no moth destroys. For where your treasure is, there your heart will be also. (Luke 12:32-34)

A review of both biblical and modern history shows that some saintly people were perpetually poor economically and some evil people became quite wealthy. The psalmist complained to God that evil people were prospering. In Psalm 10, the poet cried out in anguish about the injustice he perceived.

> The wicked boast of the desires of their heart,
> those greedy for gain curse and renounce the LORD.
> In the pride of their countenance the wicked say, "God

> will not seek it out";
>   all their thoughts are, "There is no God."
> Their ways prosper at all times.
>
> (Psalm 10:3-5a)

The dilemma echoes down through history. The popularity of the book *When Bad Things Happen to Good People*, by Harold S. Kushner, is not surprising. The biblical story of Job is a theological attempt to wrestle with that same issue. Justice is not always either instant or observable.

If there is reciprocity, what is its nature? Where does it start? Is God the one who initiates the action, to which humans reciprocate? Or do humans act and God responds/rewards? Does the blessing make possible, or at least enrich, the connection between the person and God, or does the person's action make it possible for God to bestow a blessing? If there is a connection, what is the nature of the reciprocity?

All through the witness of the Hebrew Bible, God's blessings are given in order for the recipient to be a blessing to the nations. Blessings, whether they are material or spiritual, always carry responsibility. The blessing provides the power to be a blessing. God initiates the action by blessing the person or family or nation. The person (or family or nation) is then to be a blessing to others. The blessing is not a reward but a call to mission.

Our spiritual ancestors were not of one voice on the issue of rewards and reciprocity. The Psalms express some of the painful struggles with the relationship between blessing and goodness. Psalm 73 seems to be the linchpin of the argument, standing near the center of this collection of one hundred fifty hymns of the Jewish faith. The psalmist sees bad people prospering. It doesn't seem fair. He questions how life could appear so inequitable.

> Such are the wicked;
>   always at ease, they increase in riches.
> All in vain I have kept my heart clean
>   and washed my hands in innocence.
> For all day long I have been plagued,
>   and am punished every morning.
>
> (Psalm 73:12-14)

A few verses later, the psalmist comes to the conclusion that the prosperity of the wicked is like a transitory dream (see verses 18-20). The conclusion is that true hope is not in prosperity or in things. "But for me it is good to be near God" (verse 28). God may provide tangible blessings, but the real blessing is the presence of this loving, merciful God. Nothing could be greater than to live in the presence of God.

In the book of Job, theodicy is the core issue. If God is God, why do good people suffer? It seems self-evident that in a just world, people who suffer must have been bad and people who prosper must be good. However, there are too many examples all through history of contradictions to that common wisdom. Why do such bad things happen to righteous people? Can there be any motivation for doing good other than greed or the applause of the crowd? This is the question raised by Satan

HOW DO YOU DEFINE BLESSING? IS BLESSING COUNTED IN STOCKS, BANK ACCOUNTS, AND PROPERTY? OR ARE BLESSINGS EXPERIENCED AS AN INVITATION INTO THE PRESENCE OF GOD? OR . . . ?

in verse 9 of the first chapter of Job: "Does Job fear God for nothing?" Do people ever do good without any hope of reward? Is a relationship with God enough of a reward in itself? If a reward is expected, what kind of reward is hoped for or anticipated?

Many people see giving as an act of obedience. God is experienced as the one who brings order out of the chaos of life. It is not surprising that those who have experienced that ordering believe that if you are obedient, God will bless you. Although the forthright statement in Deuteronomy 28 about God's blessings covers much more than sacrifices and giving, a basis is clearly stated that equates obedience with God's blessing:

> If you will only obey the LORD your God, by diligently observing all his commandments that I am commanding you today, the LORD your God will set you high above all the nations of the earth; all these blessings shall come upon you and overtake you, if you obey the LORD your God. (Deuteronomy 28:1-2)

When we read these words from our North American individualistic perspective, the contract seems quite straightforward. However, the text is addressed to the nation of Israel. It was corporate obedience that would bring peace to the

HOW BIG IS YOUR GOD?

nation and prosperity to the people. Of course, it is impossible to have a faithful nation without having faithful families and individuals. However, there is no quid pro quo for individuals that guarantees personal health, wealth, and happiness for keeping certain commandments.

If the Old Testament is the story of a people trying to comprehend this marvelous God who brought them out of the land of Egypt, the core issue for reciprocity is the nature of God. God is faithful. God is loving! A retired cemetery manager may have described this in his own unique way when he responded to my question about what God had to do with giving. Abe said:

> *I don't know that God has anything to do with it. I sort of believe that even if you didn't give anything, God would still be on your side. You can't buy off God.*

A god who blesses is a personal god. This god is involved in the lives of people. Perhaps one reason why some people do not feel blessed is because they have never discovered the personal God, revealed in Jesus of Nazareth. The Christian affirmation is that in Jesus the Word became flesh (John 1:14). God can no longer be the object of abstract speculation. God is not a metaphysical abstraction. God became flesh and blood in this real world.

Everything about our earthly existence is changed because of Jesus. Jesus revealed God. Our use of our giftedness and our material possessions reveals the priorities in our lives. It reveals our values. How we earn money, save money, spend money, and give money signals our real values to others. Our reaction to receiving both intangible and material gifts says a lot about who we are. Denying tangible blessings in this life may be a way of denying the Incarnation. The earthiness of the Christian faith has within its very nature an understanding of blessing.

Good things often become abused. Good things can be used for bad purposes. The temptation stories in the Synoptic Gospels do not claim that there is anything inherently wrong with having bread. Bread was broken at the last supper that Jesus ate with his disciples. Bread was broken by Jesus and the two who walked with him on the Emmaus road. However, a good thing like bread can be used for the wrong reasons. When we affirm the blessings of God, we are on track. When we attempt to manipulate God into blessing us, we bring down curses rather than blessings.

Giving is a spiritual discipline that helps us keep all the rest of life in perspective. It is not magic. It affects the nitty-gritty of life. Giving is a way of aligning ourselves with God in the midst of many temptations to wander off on our own.

Endnotes

1 Reprinted from *Plain Talk About Churches and Money*, by Dean Hoge, Patrick McNamara, and Charles Zech, by permission of the Alban Institute, Inc., 7315 Wisconsin Avenue, Suite 1250W, Bethesda, Maryland 20814-3211. Copyright © 1997. All rights reserved; page 43.

2 From *The Oxford Universal Dictionary of Historical Principles*, Third Edition (Oxford University Press, 1955); page 784.

3 From "Patterns of Giving Among United Methodists: Member Contributions to the Local Church," by Charles E. Zech, in *The People(s) Called Methodist: Forms and Reforms of Their Life* (Abingdon Press, 1998); page 92.

To Put This Chapter Into Practice

Individuals

1. Do you believe that you give primarily in order to be blessed, or do you give because you have been blessed?
2. What does the word *bless* mean to you? Ask some of your friends what the word means to them.
3. If you received the blessing of more money, what would you do with it? Would it really be a blessing?
4. When something good happens in your life, do you thank God or do you pat yourself on the back for doing so well?
5. Is *obligation* a good word or a bad word for you? Is it something that is imposed from outside, or does it well up from within you?
6. Does your understanding of reward relate to individual/family or to the community/world? What is the evidence?
7. Read the parable of the Pharisee and the tax collector in Luke 18:9-14. What kind of prayers of thanksgiving are not appropriate?

Church Leaders

1. At the next meeting of your board/committee, have the people pair up. Give the pairs seven minutes to tell each other ways they have been blessed in their lives.
2. If the people of your church were more generous in their financial giving, how would the community be blessed? Who would be blessed beyond the local community? On the basis of your answer to those two questions, what would you like to communicate to the people of your congregation who give?
3. What are some ways to celebrate blessings of the whole church or community? Make a list of kinds of blessings that are communal. Rule out any individual blessings.
4. Write four prayers of thanksgiving that do not fall into the trap of the Pharisee's prayer in Luke 18. Use one of these prayers in each worship service for a month.

6

Tithing

⟢

Bring the full tithe into the storehouse.
(Malachi 3:10)

I n a previous book, I wrote about tithing from a biblical, historical, and devotional perspective.[1] In this chapter I invite you to look at tithing through the testimony of people who hold a variety of convictions about the ancient tradition, and the rich variety of ways they endeavor to observe it. Most of the interviewees took tithing seriously, though there is a considerable variety in interpretation and practice. Some have tithed their income all of their lives. Others recently started tithing, and some aspire to move to that level of giving but are not there yet. Yes, I also met some generous folks who think tithing is a foolish concept having little to do with spiritual maturity and an unrealistic standard for giving in the present North American economy.

Tithing is one response to the question many Christian givers face when deciding how much they will give. For some of the generous givers in our churches, calculating the amount is not even a question. Tithing is "what you do" when you are a Christian. For them, tithing is God's man-dated "tax." Others consider the tithe as a norm that is as much a part of their lives as brushing their teeth or tying their shoes. For others still, it is a benchmark on the path of their striving. They strive to reach that level of giving then move beyond it. Some folks I interviewed never mentioned the T word, and a few of the generous people in this study have moved beyond tithing.

I offer to you a typology of attitudes toward tithing. There are (1) the "Brought Up Right," (2) the Strivers, (3) the Accepters, (4) the Ambivalent, and (5) the Grateful. Most of these types can be found in most congregations. They come out of different experiences. Their thought processes differ from one another. Their spiritual perspectives are not the same. While we can admire certain things about each one of the types, all have room for growth.

The "Brought Up Right"

From the point of view of many church finance leaders, some folks were simply "brought up right" to tithe. As we already pointed out, both family training and church instruction play an important role in determining whether to give at all as well as how much to give. Many people told stories about tithing as a child without ever using the word. They described getting fifty cents and putting five cents in the offering envelope. For others, tithing was a concept that was explicitly taught to them when they were children. For Mrs. Moore it encompassed more than church giving; it was a way of life that was taught in the home:

> I was taught to give. I was in a family of six children. We lived in Louisiana. And we were given two cents a piece every Sunday morning to put in Sunday school. And that was a requirement, and the teacher would know what we had. I was taught to give and to share at home with my brothers and sisters. We worked together. We were never really in need. We didn't live extravagantly, so we were taught. And then one thing I remember that—and I still do this—at a Christmas Club my mother would give us twenty-five cents a week. And we had to walk to the bank. And at Christmas time we got a little check of $12.50, and that seemed like so much money. And out of that [we] were required to give our donation to the church, buy a gift for our teacher and sisters and brothers. So we brought little simple things like pencils and things like that. We didn't have a whole lot of money. We were taught to give. It has carried through all my life. I believe in giving and sharing.

A majority of the people I interviewed were raised either with the example of tithing or with explicit instructions to tithe. However, most of them either forgot about their earlier training or brushed the practice aside during their teen years or as young adults. One of those who reclaimed the early childhood teaching later in life was an older woman from the inner city of Los Angeles. Mrs. Harrison said:

> My momma died when I was twelve years old. My grandmother raised me, and I always paid that little tithe. I called it a tip until I learned better. I did not know the

meaning of it. As I went to conferences, women's meetings, Saturday morning meet-
ings, I finally discovered what the tithe was all about. A small percentage of income
you give to the work of God. Some people call it the ten percent tithe. That's the way
I was brought up.

You will note that when she was a child, she observed an important adult figure in her life tithe. It wasn't until she began to study tithing as an adult that she found out "what [it] was all about." Her comments imply two levels of knowledge. On the first level, she was brought up to tithe even though she did not seem to know that a tithe meant ten percent. She simply learned to do it.

It may be fair to ask how one can tithe without knowing how to calculate a tithe. Conversely, it is possible to do the mathematical calculations without having the spirit of tithing. The Pharisees seemed to know how to calculate a tithe, but they did not find any connection with God in the action. When Mrs. Harrison heard tithing explained as an adult, tithing took on inner meaning as well. She connected the action with the meaning.

A former Catholic recounted his story of coming back to childhood instruction and practice as an adult. He remembered hearing about tithing as he grew up in the Catholic Church. However, the call to tithe was laden with guilt in his memory. In spite of that past history, he wanted his United Methodist church to teach tithing more aggressively—but without guilt.

There are those who claim that the instruction of a child will always come back at some point in his or her lifetime. On the other hand, some people rebel against the patterns of their youth. It is certainly hard to develop patterns later in life if they were not first introduced during one's youth. The evidence is shaky at best to prove the maxim that people who are taught to tithe as children will grow up to tithe. However, it is not unusual for childhood memories and patterns to reemerge later in life. One thing is patently clear—no single pattern fits all.

The Strivers

Quite a few of the people interviewed feel a great sense of obligation to do whatever is expected of a Christian. This attitude was more likely to be expressed by young adults than by older church members. They want to know about the next steps in their spiritual journey. Many started striving toward the tithe as the goal of their giving once they made a personal commitment to Jesus Christ. They started to read the Bible after their conversion or spiritual awakening. They looked for guidance and instruction from the written Word. They looked for a map to guide them on this part of their spiritual journey. Perhaps this was expressed no more directly than by a young man from western Virginia. He said:

My aspiration is to give ten percent. I hope I make it next year.

The aspiration is often accompanied by struggle. Some of it is financial, and some of it is in the head and heart. Tonya, a young woman from Nashville, said:

I had always been hung up or obsessed with the full ten percent. But in a sermon, the minister said that it is okay to grow to ten percent, to start somewhere and then gradually grow. So that said to me that this is something I can do. I am moving in that direction. I am trying to get there. I started at two percent and stayed at that level for about six months, moved up and saw that even with giving what I thought was a huge amount of my small amount of money that it came to me. I was able to go on and pledge the full ten percent.

It seems obvious that God constituted humans in a rich variety of formats. Some folks stick their toe into the water to test it; others dive headlong into the lake. Some make a decision and never look back. Others constantly reevaluate every decision. There are cautious strivers, and there are determined strivers.

A retired CPA in Roanoke, Virginia, seemed to characterize the determined striver. He did not describe the roots of his decision to tithe. Even so, he fits the description of a striver. Justin is a person who makes a decision and doesn't question it. He just does it. Justin described his venture into tithing with these words:

When I started tithing, the first month was terrible. The second month wasn't so bad. The third month, it became pretty routine. And after that, it had a financial impact.

When I read his comments now, I am fascinated by his observation that tithing "had a financial impact" only *after* the practice became routine. I wonder if Justin tried to keep his tithing from interfering with his other spending decisions during those first three months. It is likely that after three months of tithing, changes in lifestyle had to be made if he was to continue giving at that level. If that is the case, the decision to tithe became a force that rearranged his whole pattern of personal economic practices.

A young adult financial planner from New Jersey participated in the church's youth ministry during his teenage years, then he dropped out of church. He recently began coming to the small congregation where I interviewed him. He had heard of tithing not in his church but through his clients. Chuck noted that some of his clients gave ten percent of their income to their churches. This intrigued him, and he asked them about it.

He described to me their understanding of the biblical call to give a tithe. His pilgrimage did not stop there. His understanding of the concept of tithing continued to grow. He is on a search. He said:

> I had to ask at this church what tithing means. Nobody ever said anything about it. All I knew was the financial part of tithing. The spiritual dimension came later. In my work we always encourage people to save ten percent of their income. Now I see tithing as saving ten percent for your future—after you leave here.

Chuck observed that the act of contributing ten percent of one's money through the church is not necessarily a spiritual act. Throughout the biblical accounts, the tithe was acclaimed whenever it helped a person express a relationship with the Almighty. But tithing was condemned when it was simply a transaction done to impress others or an attempt to bargain with God.

Not all strivers have arrived at the ten percent benchmark of giving. Striving has its own reward. A young adult with two children described his struggle to reach the tithe. He was on a journey. Andrew mixed feelings of aspiration, obligation, and strategy when he said:

> My goal is to make sure I give ten percent. Probably the neat part is that when I look at the monthly budget or weekly budget, you really don't miss it. If you wait last to do it, you probably miss it. I guess that is how it ought to be done.

Striving is rarely easy. That is because it encompasses more than the act of putting money in the plate. It affects all of life. For many, it is an ongoing struggle. They work at it but may not have arrived. Ben expressed his striving without attaining when he said:

> Well, I try to think of all of the programs we are living off here, and designate the funds according to the way I feel. We have a second offering, called loose change, and that entire amount goes into our apportionments. I would say we collect forty to fifty dollars a week. That helps. Sometimes it's a struggle. I try to tithe; it is hard.

Ben's striving toward the tithe is related to his relationship with the community of faith as well as his developing connection with God. The money, others in the church, and God are all included in the struggle.

The Accepters

Duty creates rebellion from some and is a powerful motivator for others. A sense of duty may come from parental teaching, from a peer, or from reading the Scripture. The culture or the teachings of a respected adult stirs the duty button in some of my interviewees. Debbie from Chicago is an example of one who accepted the teaching of an authority figure. She learned about tithing after she became an adult. She received her encouragement to tithe while watching a popular religious television program.

I used to watch Robert Schuller on TV. I really enjoyed him a lot. He always said, "Tithe, and if you find a church, tithe to that church." In my research—of the Bible, Malachi—it said something about if you tithe as you should, the ten percent, you will be showered. I guess you could say that this is what I should be doing. It is a sense of obligation or duty.

Her words imply that she first heard about tithing from the Schuller broadcast and found the instruction confirmed by her own study of the Bible. I don't know what other things were going on in Debbie's life during that period of time. For instance, why was she drawn to religious programming? What attracted her to Robert Schuller? If we knew the answers to those questions, we would learn more about how the soil of her soul was prepared for the seed of Schuller's message. In any case, Debbie was open to accepting the authority of a popular preacher along with the authority of the Scriptures.

Most of the Korean Christians who told me their stories had an attitude toward giving (and a practice of giving) that stands in marked contrast with most Euro-Americans and African Americans. Giving ten percent seems to be taken for granted. They do not even consider working toward it. They accept the tithe as a place to start. One aspect of being a Christian is to tithe—period. What is there to debate?

However, paying close attention to a mathematical percentage does not take the place of spontaneous giving in the Korean-American culture. Mark, a young parent in a southern California Korean congregation, was fairly typical of the Koreans I interviewed. He said:

Ten percent is just basic. I stopped counting. Whatever the Holy Spirit tells me to do in my heart, I do it. The amount or what percentage—I don't think that is what is important. I always pray to God, "Let this ten percent increase." And I tell God, "Give me the faith and heart to give more than I am giving."

Notice that Mark did not ask God to give him more money but more "faith and heart." Many of the Korean Christians I interviewed believe that tithing is a key that opens the door to greater generosity. When Euro-Americans hear the word *tithe*, many hear it as a burden and label it as legalism. The Korean-American Christians I interviewed did not perceive the tithe as an encumbrance. For them, it is the name of a friend at the starting point of a spiritual journey. It is not a friend that you decide whether or not to invite along. This racial-ethnic group simply accepts the fact that this friend, the tithe, is a part of their faith journey.

Gospel stories show that the act of tithing does not automatically make a person generous from the heart. Jesus condemned the tithing Pharisees who neglected justice and mercy while holding fast to the practice of tithing (see Matthew 23:23.) In another Jesus story, two men went into the Temple to pray. The one who tithed received the condemnation of Jesus rather than the commendation (Luke 18:9-14).

For one person, the sense of duty came with her marriage vows. I asked Rachel, "How do you decide how much you are going to give?" Her response was straightforward:

> Well, I think it is decided by my husband. He gives the tithes. We try to stick with the ten percent. My husband has a share in the business. It is doing real well. We pretty much know what we can give each week.

Although my interview sample included only generous Christians, apparently few generous Americans from a European ancestry tithe.[2] Many people who were scheduled for interviews because they were generous givers saw themselves on the way toward that goal. In fact, they accepted the tithe as an objective to work toward. A few of them even considered the tithe as another pie-in-the-sky ideal that someone came up with but that is totally outside the realm of possibility for most people. We now turn to that group.

The Ambivalent

Where the benchmark of the tithe is seen as an important and positive value, it is an expression of one's relationship with God. However, it is not a simple quid pro quo deal with God. Some of the people were not sure about it. A young mother from Missouri recognized the choices involved in tithing. Although she and her husband made the decision to give ten percent, there seemed to be a bit of mental equivocation about the decision. In response to a question about tithing, Gloria responded:

> I do worry about putting the kids through college. We have two. That's more of a worry than my retirement right now.

Others may want to tithe but feel economically prevented from doing so. When a person feels very strapped for money and feels that tithing is an obligation, the result can often be described as hedging. Mental ambivalence is expressed. The consequence is often to search for some other way to fulfill the responsibility. Quite often, that other way is to make up for the financial deficit by donating time. A Boomer who has a fairly small income considers himself a handy man. He said:

> When I became a member of this church, this church had a very strong drive every year as far as the stewardship drive. That is probably when I began my practice [of

giving]. Probably in the last five years or even longer, while I may not be giving a total financial tithe (ten percent to this church), I try to make it up in providing free labor for the church. I think when you add the two together . . .

Not all of the people who are ambivalent about tithing are in difficult financial straights. A fairly well-to-do woman in southern California said:

For my own thinking, I don't believe in tithing, per se. I gave more than the tithe recently. But I don't set out to do that, in a way, so in that sense I am not making that kind of commitment.

Rose went on to say that the feeling a person gets from giving is more important than the amount he or she gives. She implied that rigid devotion to a percentage can diminish the spiritual meaning. The struggle to tithe and the struggle for the meaning of all giving are not totally unrelated.

The Grateful

A middle-aged couple in California talked about their sense of being among the economically fortunate. Ned Scott said:

I guess I just feel that we are very, very fortunate in what we have been able to accomplish financially over the years. I don't feel the least bit bad about giving some of it back. I don't know if it has a lot to do with it, but I think about my Methodist minister brother who is poor. I never felt like I needed anyone to talk me into giving more.

As you may be able to tell, Ned's statement was in response to a question about church financial campaigns. He didn't need anyone to tell him he was grateful (or supposed to be grateful). He considered himself very fortunate. He was grateful and gave out of that gratitude. The gratitude was heightened by the contrast between his own financial condition and the economic situation of a brother he admired.

It is clear that simply knowing about tithing does not cause a person to tithe. If a person is grateful, she or he may tithe without ever sitting down and calculating what a tithe is. However, few people tithe unless they have heard of tithing. After people come to a new relationship with Christ and the church, they look at the implications for every aspect of their lives. In this sense, their gratitude is not for blessings from God but simply for the knowledge that God loves them and has saved them.

This understanding was illustrated by a group of local church leaders from a Hispanic church in Ventura, California, who sat at a table and talked with me for over an hour. One of the men said,

Actually, I did not come to Christ until just before I came to this church. I always knew about ten percent tithing, but I never participated in that at all—until I came

to this church. And I think that [I started] because of my tutor, my sister-in-law.
She taught me about tithing.

His sister-in-law taught him about tithing, but he already knew about tithing. It seems clear that teaching went far beyond imparting information. His decision to tithe had roots, but it also had a boost. He was not open to accept the teaching or to respond to the opportunity until he experienced the "coming to Christ." Tithing became one of the ways he responded to the new life he found in Christ.

One of the most interesting comments came from Brad in Rhode Island, who said that he did not believe in tithing.

We don't set out to give a tithe. Last year [we gave] double the tithe. We are not the biggest proportional givers in the church. When incomes go up, it is much easier to be generous.

It seems likely that Brad reacts against a rigid mathematical rule but affirms the generosity of response that does not keep score. At the same time, note that he did keep score. While claiming to pay no attention to the tithe, he was aware that he gave "double the tithe."

Calculating the Tithe

How much is a tithe? What is the basis for the mathematical calculation? Faithful people have struggled and argued about the way to compute the amount for hundreds of years. The tithe is figured in many different ways. A common question is, Is it figured on the net or the gross? For these questioners, tithing becomes mathematical number crunching based on cash income.

However, determining ten percent of one's income was not the route for everyone interviewed. A middle-class couple from Los Angeles had their own unique way of figuring out how much to give. Dianne described it in this way:

Well, when he was working, we made a point that if we could give fifteen percent to a restaurant when you tip somebody, you could give fifteen percent to the church. We decided that if you were going to tip somebody else, you might as well tip God.

Since Dianne's husband, Felix, retired, they cut back on the percentage of the financial giving, but they are now able to contribute a lot of time and skill to the ministries of the church.

For others, time is included (or rationalized) in the process of calculation. I found the inclusion of time especially important for younger adults. Bruce Kim described giving in this way:

Giving means many things to me. In order to give something, your heart has to be prepared. Giving only exists when there is movement in your heart. So, church giving means not just financially, but also your devotion of time and also your caring and also [giving] toward others.

A young Native American was quite blunt about the importance of time in the equation when she said:

Giving my time is an investment of myself. Giving money is an easy way out.

A similar viewpoint was expressed by Candace in Rhode Island. She said:

Giving of time was just as important as giving myself and just as valid. Even when I don't have a lot financially, I give of myself. Even now I feel that what I give in time and other things is just as important [as giving money].

Patricia, a middle-aged woman in Virginia, described a difference, yet a connection, between tithing money and giving time. She said:

The church check is one of the first checks I write each month. We tithe. If special things come up, I give. It is one way to give beyond ten percent. I am very involved in district projects like committee work and work camps at Alta Mont. Some people from the congregation have gone on a VIM [Volunteers in Mission] project to Haiti. A group from here went to help in the flood relief in Missouri. This kind of work is over and above the tithe.

Brenda, another woman from Rhode Island, reflected this relationship between time and giving with a fascinating description of her attitudes toward retirement. She tried to express how her values changed and how those values were reflected in her total giving. She articulated her priorities in a negative sort of way when she said:

If you can retire early, then you can do the leisure things you want to do. That is awfully wound up in itself—and that is debilitating, I think, spiritually.

GIVING IS AN EXPRESSION OF A RELATIONSHIP RATHER THAN AN EFFORT TO BUILD A RELATIONSHIP.

Her concern is spiritual health. When the inner self is focused on one's relationship with God, it is reflected in giving. For Brenda, moving into a mathematical calculation was neither the goal of her life nor an expression of her relationship with God. It went far deeper than that. Her giving was an expression of a relationship rather than an effort to build a relationship. It seems clear that for some givers, the tithe is a response flowing out of their experience of God's love and/or power. For others, it is a visible signpost on the road of their spiritual journey. God is not limited to one way of nurturing people.

Deeper Roots

The prophets of the Old Testament railed against those who brought tithes and sacrifices to the Temple but failed to bring justice and mercy to the land. Every act of sacrifice and giving was to be a sign of a relationship. In one sense, every act of giving is a sign, but of what? Jesus confronted the tension when he said, "Woe to you, scribes and Pharisees, hypocrites! For you tithe mint, dill, and cumin, and have neglected the weightier matters of the law: justice and mercy and faith" (Matthew 23:23).

Matthew described a whole series of denunciations of the scribes and Pharisees in chapter 23. Jesus assailed those who

> do all their deeds to be seen by others; for they make their phylac-teries broad and their fringes long. They love to have the place of honor at banquets and the best seats in the synagogues, and to be greeted with respect in the marketplaces, and to have people call them rabbi. (Matthew 23:5-7)

When the motivation for tithing was to strut one's piousness in public, it was condemned. When tithing was an act of gratitude or relationship, it was affirmed.

In the Sermon on the Mount, Jesus said much the same thing:

> Whenever you give alms, do not sound a trumpet before you, as the hypocrites do in the synagogues and in the streets, so that they may be praised by others. Truly I tell you, they have received their reward. But when you give alms, do not let your left hand know what your right hand is doing, so that your alms may be done in secret; and your Father who sees in secret will reward you. (Matthew 6:2-4)

Giving is to be a reflection of the core of one's life. When it is only a veneer, it is an abomination. A new center in a person's life changes the outward actions. However, people are perfectly able to perform outer changes without anything happening to the core of their being. Many others, however, have acknowledged how a new practice leads to a change of heart. Outward changes sometimes lead to inward transformation. Tithing may force a person to deeply examine basic values.

Attitudes toward God and the church may have far more to do with practices than we imagined. Attitudes are shaped by a host of childhood experiences and influences. We may be missing the point when we talk about "motivating people to give." Motivations are written deeply within the hearts and souls of people. Why do some people want to join the church primarily for the fellowship and other people because they are desperately seeking a relationship with God? Every seeker has a story, or a combination of stories.

At the beginning of the twenty-first century, tithing is counter-cultural. It may be the supreme means of thumbing our nose at the demonic power of consumerism. "We look not at what can be seen but at what cannot be seen; for what can be seen is temporary, but what cannot be seen is eternal" (2 Corinthians 4:18). When we determine to give away at least ten percent, we are signaling to ourselves and to others that we march to a different drummer.

Summary

Some people accept tithing as a challenge and describe it in warm terms. Others see it as a challenge but are frustrated because they have not attained the goal. They tend to be the hard-driving Christians who will grit their teeth and do what is required. At best, for this group the goal of tithing is like that of a coach on the sidelines urging them to keep running the race. Too often, the predominant emotion of these givers is guilt about not attaining the goal rather than joy at the oppor-tunity to be in the race.

People become part of the faith community for a variety of reasons. They also move from the starting point in a myriad of directions. Some peo-ple seem to feel that they have done their duty to God by joining a church. They view generous giving of time and money as a special calling meant only for the very religious. Tithing ranks up there with celibacy and monas-tic life as an unattainable ideal. It may be good for a few, but they don't really believe that God expects it from "normal" people.

Tithing is not a political contribution to gain access to the higher power. The tithe is more like a sign along the spiritual roadway than it is a way of bribing God to do what we want. It is part and parcel of the faith journey. A Boomer parent in Virginia described his movement toward tithing as an attempt to take faith more seriously. He said:

> I tried to do what I could—after I paid my bills. I probably gave what was left or what I felt comfortable with. In the last five or six years we have tried to make a commitment to set aside the church's [portion] first, rather than last. My goal is to make sure I give ten percent. Then I can say I'm giving my full tithe.

The tithe is a visible symbol of putting first things first. In fact, many tithers spoke about setting aside the tithe as the first act of their financial accounting. Some mentioned the encouragement of Paul to the Corinthians that "on the first day of every week, each of you is to put aside and save whatever extra you earn" (1 Corinthians 16:2). Generous givers find that giving "off the top" is both more helpful to their own financial management and a more joyful way to contribute to spreading the message of Jesus. Some use the Old Testament terminology of "first fruits" giving as a way to describe their practice. It is also a way of reminding the giver of God's care about the totality of life. Tithing is not a flippant act.

Endnotes

1 See *Holy Smoke! Whatever Happened to Tithing?* By J. Clif Christopher and Herb Mather (Discipleship Resources, 1999).

2 See *Behind the Stained Glass Window: Money Dynamics in the Church*, by John and Sylvia Ronsvalle (Baker Books, 1996); page 335.

To Put This Chapter Into Practice

Individuals

1. Think through your own feelings about tithing. If you tithe your income, do you do so out of duty, or is it spontaneous? Did you start out of duty and move toward more spontaneous giving?
2. If you do not presently tithe, work out a personal or family budget with ten percent coming off the top. What adjustments would have to be made in your lifestyle?

Church Leaders

1. Bring a group of parents of young children together to discuss how they decide how much to give to their children to put in the offering plate. Provide guidance to this discussion with information about the biblical and historical practice of tithing.
2. Invite a group of receptive people from your congregation to participate in a thirty-day experience for learning how to practice the discipline of tithing found in the book *Holy Smoke! Whatever Happened to Tithing?* (Discipleship Resources, 1999). The process is described on pages 55–61 of *Holy Smoke!*, with daily Scripture readings and questions for thought on pages 91–108.

7

The Offering

The Scene: After the organist played a vigorous Bach composition, the people who gathered at First Church on Sunday were called to worship by a liturgist. The liturgist read selected verses from Psalm 100 to the congregation. Then the congregation sang hymns, read prayers, and heard a leader offer a prayer on their behalf. They listened to the choir sing an anthem. They listened to the reading of Scripture lessons and to a sermon preached. The bulletin indicated that it was now time for the offering.

A pastor stepped to the lectern and read: ". . . Remembering the words of the Lord Jesus Christ, how he said, 'It is more blessed to give than to receive,' let us now offer our tithes and offerings to the Lord. Will the ushers wait upon us for our morning offerings?"

Pre-selected people, chosen to be the collectors for that particular Sunday, synchronized their march down the aisles. They carried beautifully shined metallic plates in front of them. The plates had circles of dark green felt in the bottom. Starting at the first pew in which people were sitting, the collectors passed the plates back and forth so that everyone in the congregation had the opportunity to place something in a plate.

When all the collectors completed their task and returned to the back of the church, the organist struck a chord. The congregation stood and the collectors marched down the center aisle. All joined in singing the Doxology: "Praise God, from whom all blessings flow . . ." The collectors presented the plates to the pastor, who turned toward the altar, lifted them high, and offered a prayer of dedication.

This common scene in Protestant churches in North America may have a hazy connection to the tradition of the Catholic Mass. In the Mass, the priest lifts the host and prays a Eucharistic prayer. The elements of bread and wine become the body and blood of Christ. While there is more to Catholic Eucharistic theology than I can go into here, the connection I wish to make is that the elements are transformed (transubstantiated) into the sacrificial presence of Christ in the midst of the congregation. The gifts of the people are brought into the presence of God, and the supreme gift of God is now in the presence of the people. This whole portion of the Mass is called the Offertory.

In the Protestant church where I worshiped as a child, we had a time in worship called "The Offertory" in the bulletin. At that point in the service, the financial offering was collected from the worshipers. The collectors brought it to the front of the church, where the funds were placed on the altar table and dedicated. At some point in Protestant history, the financial offering of the people seems to have replaced the offering of Jesus on the cross, symbolized by the offering of bread and wine.

When financial offerings are dedicated, the prayer is that the money given by the people will be transformed into Christ's ministry in the world. Transformation of the money into ministry does not take place in the worship service so much as it does when it is used in the community and throughout the world. The money given by the people makes it possible to proclaim the good news, feed the hungry, and participate in other ministries of justice and mercy.

In the Catholic tradition, the sacrificial death of Jesus is the focus of the Eucharist. The Eucharistic Mass emphasizes what God has done for us in Jesus Christ. Sometimes the Mass is referred to as "the sacrifice of the Mass." It is no wonder that Catholic stewardship conference speakers connect the financial offering to the sacrificial gift of Jesus Christ on the cross. The term *sacrificial giving* is consistently used to describe the financial offerings of the people. Even in the Catholic Church, there is a thread that connects the sacrifice of the Mass with the giving of the people.

Perhaps the biggest difference between the Mass and Protestant worship is that in Protestant worship, the offering

MODERN WORSHIP TENDS TO IGNORE THE WORD SACRIFICE. MANY CHURCHES CONSIDER DROPPING THE OFFERING FROM THEIR WORSHIP. IS SOMETHING IMPORTANT LOST WHEN THE OFFERING IS NOT A CENTRAL ACT OF WORSHIP?

is hardly the center of worship. The primary act in most Protestant congregations is the proclamation of the Word. An appreciation of the centrality of the sacraments is growing in Protestantism, but they are not commonly experienced as the most significant act of worship.

The time of offering can become a sacramental moment in worship in all churches. It can be another time when God's grace is communicated to the worshiper and those who worship can acknowledge that gift through their own giving.

In the United Methodist recommended basic pattern for worship, the offering of money becomes the worshiper's response to what God has done rather than the celebration of Christ's sacrifice. God's action and human response are not exclusive compartments that have no room for the other emphasis. Catholic worship emphasizes what God has done. North American Protestant worship is more likely to emphasize the human response to what God has done in Jesus Christ. Indeed, in one sense God's action is not complete without human response.

Placement of the Offering in Worship

Even the placement of the offering in the flow of a worship service communicates meaning. When the offering is before the reading of the Holy Scriptures and the proclamation of the Word (as in many Protestant services), it feels like it is a task to get out of the way before plunging into the *really* important part of the worship. When the offering is near the close of the service, it is more likely to be understood and experienced as part of the flow of worship. It is an act of response by the worshiper. It is part of the time of commitment and dedication of one's self.

Raymond, a Texas layperson, described the issue of placement of the offering when he said:

> Our minister has made an emphasis of it [the offering]. We used to count the offering literally during the service. It used to be early in the service. The first Scripture might be read and the offering taken, then the Gospel be read. It was very early in the service, and our minister has pushed it back fairly late in the service. It has become more of a time of thought, really a part of the worship service. [It] is a time of reflection. I think coming later in the service as it does now has made it a little more integral part, and not just time to pass the offering plate.

I wanted to know what that moment in the worship service meant to the generous people that I interviewed. Raymond was the only one to comment on the placement of the offering in the flow of the worship service. As with the other questions I posed to the generous givers, the responses to the inquiries about the offering included a rich variety of explanations. For some, the offering is a brief interlude during worship. For others, it is a high and holy moment. Some feel like it is the only time when they truly participate in worship.

I attended worship in two churches of different denominations where the worship leader announced that the offering plates were being passed so that the members could contribute to the ministries of the church. Visitors were invited to sit back, relax, and listen to the music and feel no compulsion to place anything in the plates. These seeker-sensitive services acknowledge the uneasiness of people about money and try to lessen the pressure. A question needs to be raised: Does this kind of comment communicate that the offering is simply an action taken in order to pay bills rather than an act of worship?

The Offering as Worship

A few people indicated that they are grateful that they are able to participate financially in this act of worship. For instance, a former welfare mom described the offering during a worship service as an important moment in her life:

> I think that beside Communion, it is one of the most important times of the service. To be able to share that—it just gives me an opportunity to feel that joy that I talked about. Every offering that we give, we pray. That's pretty much it—a sense of blessing.

Notice the linkage between giving, prayer, and joy. In serious contrast to this welfare mother is the comment of a twentysomething living in an affluent suburb in western Missouri. When asked about the offering in worship, Crystal wandered around in a verbal wilderness for a while before concluding that it was a good thing.

> Well, I wouldn't say it is a downer. . . . I just see it as "you have come to a good service, now this is a way for you to give in support of that good work." I would not say it is a celebration. I would say that [it] is more of an obligation. I think obligation is a neutral word. I think if you feel in control of it, it is a good word. If you feel like you are being pressured, and it is out of your control . . . I think it is negative that way. But I think the offering is more of a "I am in control of it," so it is a good thing.

In a way, Crystal took me on a tour of the feelings and attitudes whirling around in her brain before she finally got to her conclusion. The first part of her response fits the popular notion that young adults do not give—they "pay for services." Under the conventional wisdom about the Postmodern generation, young adults do not give out of gratitude or out of any desire to connect with God. They give because they feel that religion is important and they know that everything has an economic component. Therefore, in order to have a nice church and a good Sunday school and all the other things that are part of church life, someone has to pay for them. The prevailing wisdom is that young adults know they have to pay to have those things, and they will do their share just as they would expect to pay to go to a concert or play.

However, Crystal dug deeper. Control seemed to be a major issue for her. Many young adults feel out of control in much of their lives. She did not desire to control others, but she wanted to bring her own chaotic life under control. Life is not under control unless a person has finances under control. The offering becomes a time to focus on bringing the economic dimension of one's life under control. The guidance of the church and the mediation of the Holy Spirit are resources that the church rarely relates to the rough and tumble of financial survival in the real world.

DOES YOUR CHURCH OFFER TRAINING IN FINANCIAL MANAGEMENT AND SPIRITUAL SUPPORT TO THOSE WHO FEEL CALLED TO EXERCISE FAITH-CENTERED CONTROL OVER THEIR FINANCES?

Only about half of the generous people I interviewed claimed that the offering was a meaningful time of worship for them. For many, it was simply part of the action of the service, and hardly an act of connecting with God. This was especially true for Ernie, an usher in a Rhode Island congregation:

I am an usher, so it is kind of a mechanical need for me—something I have to do.

I do not wish to be judgmental about Ernie's remark. Many pastors feel that they must pay so much attention to the details of the worship service that they miss experiencing the mysterious presence of the Holy One. Attention to detail by some people helps free others to focus on God. Ernie wanted to do things right.

Few would make a claim that the act of making an offering is the high point of the worship service. In fact, one person discounted the action fairly directly:

The offering? I guess at that time, I'm not thinking about the offering.

It is clear that not all people sitting in the pews experience the offering as a holy moment. When I asked the question about the meaning of the offering to an affluent California couple who give more than a tithe, Mrs. Copeland laughed. She described the time in the worship service when the offering is taken. Her attitude was expressed with this comment:

OK. Now I don't need to walk it down to the office or put it in the mail. It is not that I think it's a bad thing. I never feel like I am required to give. We don't put something in the offering plate every Sunday. There is no feeling that, "Gee, everybody is watching so I have to put something in the plate." But it is not a religious experience either. We are not contemplating what we are going to give because we have already written the check.

Note that the decision about the amount to give and the action of writing the check seemed to be more significant than the action of offering the money within the service of worship. I wondered if the ancient Israelites had the same range of experiences and attitudes as North Americans at the dawn of the twenty-first century. The Hebrew offerings were given annually rather than weekly. The task of preparing to go to Jerusalem (or another designated shrine) annually was a major operation. It took planning. The logistics were monumental. Pilgrims had to select animals for the sacrifice. They loaded the grain and oil onto carts or directly on the backs of beasts of burden. It was a more monumental task than a twenty-first-century American planning a two-week vacation to England. Was the preparation a spiritually enriching experience for them? We don't know. The Scriptures do not tell us.

Some of the people interviewed recognized a dimension of giving related to the corporate act of worship. However, it is not something that many of them sat around and reflected upon. They experienced the offering as part of their worship but were unable to articulate the connection when asked. One person summed it up when he said:

Every week we pay. It is important that we participate in the service each week. I guess it is important that we put something in the offering plate each week.

Participating in the offering is something folks do when they go to worship, but it is not one of the times when most worshipers recognize a connection between themselves and God. Even among many generous givers, the offering is often a break in the service in order to collect the funds for the institution rather than an act of worship.

For others, it is a time for meditation. Even in those cases, they are more apt to think about the needs of others than the sacrifice of God. It may be the moment in worship when some people have a broader focus than "me and God." In fact, meditation may be a time for God to speak to us about others of God's creatures in the world. For some, the offering is a time to recognize that there are those with little to give. Another Californian gave his thoughts on the offering by saying:

Every time, especially offering time, in my mind, I think there is a lot of people out there who are not able to . . . clothe or feed themselves. But God has given me this abundance—financial—so I don't have to worry about that. So I thank God for that. I hold that offering and I say, "Thank you, God, for giving me such opportunity to give you ten percent to use for your work." I try to make a habit of at least pulling something out of my pocket. I think it is good to let others see you giving something. You are setting somewhat of a precedent. They don't know how much it is.

Most clergy leaders would like to have their people more informed about the history and traditions of worship. There may be a counter danger. If we are able to explain everything that happens in worship, the mechanics of worship can distract us and cause us to lose sight of the one who is greater than any of our attempts to structure an experience of encounter. Some people experience God in spite of poorly designed worship and in spite of the fact that they have no knowledge of the biblical and historical roots. However, the question must be raised: Do people have a hard time connecting faith and money because we have designed worship to disconnect them from its roots and from one another?

Perhaps the offering is not unique in this way. Few worshipers reflect upon the meaning of any specific movements or aspects of the worship service. Why do we sing hymns? Why read or recite an affirmation of faith? Why are paraments on the altar? What is the tradition and meaning behind the benediction? We could go on and on with these kinds of questions. It is part of what we do when we come to worship.

Consider the extensive act of selection and preparation of our Hebrew forebears as they prepared to go to the Temple when the offerings were sacrificed annually. The Bible does not describe the process the givers went through in preparation. Many accounts are recorded about the act of making the sacrifice in the Temple. Detailed directions are given for sacrifices and offerings. The central act of worship for the Hebrews was the sacrifice. It was to be done decently and in order.

At its best, the time of offering is a time when the giver acknowledges something bigger than oneself. The offering is an act of participation in the world and in the lives of others. It is an acknowledgement that life is more than consuming. Honor may be present in the giving of money.

At the end of a weeklong seminar in Malawi, Africa, the participants gave each of us who were the leaders a gift. The gift was not simply given. It was presented not with speeches but with a parade. The women in the Malawi church formed a long line and slowly brought the gifts from the back of the room to the front, where we were standing. They came with singing. As they sang, they rhythmically walked from the back to the front of the room carrying the beautifully wrapped gifts in front of them. The gift bearers stood in front of the three of us who had come to them from America. The singing continued. My knees were weak. I have never felt so honored in my life.

As I reflect upon that experience now, I wonder if God feels honored when we offer our gifts in a service of worship. Can the time of the offering in a worship service be a time of honoring God?

A Time of Centering

For some, the offering is a time of reflection and centering. A middle-aged woman in Sepulvada, California, described what she does when the offering is received. She said:

When the ushers go up, I start praying, thanking God for things that are meaning-ful to me, and for guiding me. I say little things like that. It is very spiritual to me.

Another person, Gene, from the same church expressed the following:

At this church I really feel it is a very religious experience. We have a very heavy wooden cross that is extended from the ceiling. It is directly above the altar. When the ushers put the plate on the altar, most people, including myself, look up to the cross.

When Gene identified the cross with the offering, he was not describing the cross in the manner of "a cross to bear." Perhaps this statement comes closer to the attitudes of the Hebrew sacrifice than any other comment I heard during the interviews. A pastor of an inner-city church in the Midwest said the cross is important to the people of his church because they have such a difficult life. "It reminds them that they are not in it all alone."

For those who do find the offering meaningful, the most common response is that the offering is a time for quiet and meditation. It is an opportunity within the liturgy for spiritual daydreaming. Walter, a young man in a church located in a poor neighborhood of Chicago, expressed his appreciation for the offering in this way:

I find it a time to meditate, to maybe see myself. I would like to take the time as quiet time.

He went on to add that the appreciation he had for the quiet of that moment was tempered by the sense that something was missing.

The children are not up here when we take the collection. We don't take the collection like we used to. I think we should have the children here so they can be a part of this.

In the two parts of Walter's story we see conflicting values. If the children are in the service when the offering is taken, they participate and may grasp something of the meaning of the act. However, if they are in the service, the opportunity for the offering to be a "quiet time" may be diminished.

A Time of Celebration

In an African American church in Los Angeles, gratitude is expressed in the whole movement of the offering. With a gleam in her eye, LaTasha described that moment in their worship service in this way:

I always think: I wish that those plates would overflow. We have a practice here that when the minister announces it is time for the offering, we applaud. It is a time to be happy that we have something to give. God has given us so much that if we can't give him back something for the ministry that we are doing here at this church, then it is not doing very good of it.

When LaTasha said that God had given them so much, she was not defining the church as a group of well-to-do people. While some people in the congregation have solid middle-class incomes, more of the congregation would be listed as poor than affluent. Joy in giving is not the prerogative of any one economic class!

Cultural differences are reflected in the responses. It is quite common in African American congregations for the people to come forward to place money in the offering plates. That is rarely done in old-line, predominantly Euro-American congregations. In contrast, you should hear someone from Tonga speak animatedly of the drama in their *misinale* offering. Tongan congregations celebrate giving through an annual ingathering called a *misinale*. All year, individuals and groups gather funds for the great celebration, an exciting festival filled with singing, dancing, and giving. All give their best to God. This tradition comes closer to the celebration described in Deuteronomy 14 than any other custom that I know about.

In Africa, the offering is often received with the people beating drums, singing, and rhythmically carrying their gifts to the altar. Clapping when the offering is announced was affirmed in two churches where I interviewed people, but that action would feel like a strange interruption in most other churches in North America. The point is not to say, "Here is a way to put drama into the offering" but to invite the people of a faith community to find ways that are appropriate in its culture to help the act of giving become more meaningful.

There is a relationship between one's perspective on abundance and one's attitude toward wealth. How one feels about money in general cannot be separated from how one feels about making an offering in a worship service. A grandparent from northern Texas mused about her philosophy of money in these words:

The people that live next door to you and make $1,000 less than you do seem to get by. At the same time, people who live on the other side and make $1,000 more may have just as tough a time as you do. It is perspective.

105

Perhaps this grandmother had discovered the truth of Paul's counsel to Timothy: "There is great gain in godliness combined with contentment; for we brought nothing into the world, so that we can take nothing out of it" (1 Timothy 6:6-7).

The No-Plate Offering

The older generations of North Americans have historically paid their bills with cash or personal check. It is no wonder that these same people have made their offerings in church in the same manner. Even though Baby Boomers are more likely to pay for most things with credit cards, churches rarely offer that option. For most Boomers, using plastic doesn't seem right as a method of giving for the work of Christ. Many of them feel a bit guilty about all the bills they have racked up on their cards. To add the church "bill" to the credit card may seem too much.

Now a new generation is coming along that does not seem to have the same financial hang-ups as previous generations. Each year an increasing number of people pay their bills through electronic funds transfer (EFT). Many church members pay their YMCA or YWCA memberships through EFT. Many contribute to mutual fund accounts and pay numerous other bills by the same method. The money is automatically transferred out of their bank account and deposited directly into the account of the business or institution. Although church finance committees are dominated by older people who prefer to give through a check, an increasing number of churches across America seem willing to offer their people the option of giving through electronic funds transfer (EFT). When people choose that option, it creates interesting feelings about the act of receiving offerings during the worship service.

> I kind of feel guilty about the offering. Last year we signed up for automatic deduction of our credit card. So it always comes out. But it is not something that when the offering plate comes by you, you are putting something in. Last year we were giving to a campaign and we kind of feel like when there are new people sitting around us, we feel like when the plate is passed we should set an example or something so people will not look at us and say, "Well, they are not giving." But I try to think that is between us and God, what we give.

The "selling point" for EFT in the church is that it assures the congregation of a regular stream of money. The money comes in whether or not the person is in church that Sunday. Every month of the year, the funds are transferred, so there is no summer slump in giving. The big reservation to this method of giving is related to the meaning of the offering as an act of worship.

Special Offerings and Capital Campaigns

I asked many people about their attitudes toward special offerings. Responses tended to fall along generational lines. Older people rarely appreciate special offerings. They consider them a nuisance bordering on arm-twisting. Older folks, particularly those on finance committees, seem to desire fewer special offerings. Younger adults have the opposite reaction. They appreciate the opportunity to give to special causes. Some of the causes are very dear to them. For instance, if news programs and newspapers are filled with news about a major disaster, the younger people appreciate the opportunity to give specifically to that need.

For the most part, designated giving is more an issue for the affluent than for the poor. For instance, the poor have little to give to a capital funds campaign, while the affluent are courted for major contributions by both churches and secular organizations. Funds contributed to a capital campaign are designated giving. These funds normally come out of the accumulated assets of church members rather than from current income. Giving out of accumulation was not a focus of this study.

Regardless of whether the offerings are regular offerings for ongoing ministries, capital campaigns, or special offerings to relieve human suffering, attitudes toward the offerings are shaped by life experiences. Some people formed the habit of placing money in the offering plate each Sunday when they were children. For many of them, the time of offering is just something that is done. They continue the habit without much reflection. Others find the offering an awkward time in the service. They are uncertain about the proper response they should make as a part of this faith community.

Fifty-two Sundays each year, church leaders have an opportunity to relate the gift of God's love to the economic life of the people in the act of the offering. It can be a high and holy moment. For most congregations, that kind of result will take lots of imagination and effort.

To Put This Chapter Into Practice

Individuals

1. Plan ahead. What do you want to concentrate on when you place your offering in the plate? while the offering is being received from others? when the offering is dedicated at the altar of the church?

Church Leaders

1. At your next meeting of the finance committee, set aside twenty minutes to brainstorm about ways to make the offering meaningful if everyone in the nation stopped using cash and checks. All funds for the mission and ministry of the church could be received only by electronic funds transfer or by credit or debit cards. Could a time in the service be established that remembered the ancient sacrificial offering of the Hebrew ancestors? If the committee cannot come up with any ideas, take the puzzle to the youth group and ask them to propose suggestions.

2. Within your committee, ask the following questions: What do you get out of participation in this congregation? What does God have to do with your answer to the first question? Debrief the experience. What have you learned? How would you restate the questions?

3. Ask the two revised questions from above to people within the congregation. At your next meeting, discuss what you can learn from the responses you receive.

8

Some End-of-the-Book Observations

~~~~~

I n the Introduction of this book, the reader was advised that the stories of generosity by generous givers raise more questions than answers. Church leaders with responsibilities in finance undoubtedly recognize the complex mixture of motives behind generous giving. That is not a reason to despair; it is a sign of hope. God is greater than any of us can comprehend. God works with a diverse assortment of human beings in which no one person is the whole picture. Nor can one person see the whole picture.

There are no rabbits in the hat to solve the issue of funding the church's mission and ministry. This book is not about hat tricks. It is a snapshot of God's marvelous interaction with a variety of God's generous people. It does not tell us how to do church fundraising. The task of the congregation's financial leaders, though, is not primarily about funding. The task is one of spiritual development.

Formation is a popular subject for study in many areas of human development. Books have been written about the ways pupils learn, about the evolution of ethical values, and about spiritual maturation. I know of no books that describe the formative process in generosity. While that is not what this book is about, I hope it will contribute to a more in-depth study of the factors that foster generosity in people. In this chapter, you will find a summary of the primary ways in which spiritual formation and generosity interact as seen through the eyes of one hundred twenty-five generous givers.

The Central Role of Adult Modeling

Children are strongly influenced by the adults who are closest to them. That is the overwhelming evidence drawn from the testimonies of generous givers. Usually the primary influence is a parent. Grandparents and other significant adults in the life of a child often play a key role in the formation of values and the practice of generosity. When children grow up, they may neglect giving and sharing for a few years. Even so, nearly all of the generous givers named an influential adult during their childhood who had a major influence on their present benevolent practices.

Not every generous adult was taught to give money to a church (or anywhere else, for that matter) when a child. Even so, generous adults experienced giving and sharing by a significant older person during their formative years. They can name the person and describe the influential action. The modeling may have been a gift of time or an act of sacrificial love. Some generous givers told of observing a parent give, even though the giving was not related to the church offering. The recollections ranged from the admiration of parents who took food to the needy to an awe-filled description of a single parent who worked long hours to keep the family unit together. Others told stories of an adult who gave them the gift of time and attention.

CARING ADULTS MAKE A DIFFERENCE IN THE LIVES OF CHILDREN.

Church-related giving has many variations. Some people remember their first set of offering envelopes when they were children. Receiving the box of envelopes was a rite of passage. Others told of observing their parents prepare the church envelope every Sunday. For them, it was part of a Sunday morning ritual. Rituals communicate at a level deeper than words.

In the first fifty years of the twentieth century, nuclear families provided most of the mentoring and modeling. In the United States of America at the beginning of the twenty-first century, thirty percent of births occur to unmarried women. Many homes are blended homes, where children live with a parent and a stepparent. In some homes where there are "2 parents, 2.3 children, and a dog," the examples that children observe within the household are based on a model of acquiring rather than sharing. This book is not the place to argue about the definition of a family or to decry the morals of the nation. Blaming is rarely (never?) helpful.

Instead of bemoaning what was not done in the past, church leaders can begin creative actions that are possible now. Parents and other loving adults need tools so that they can more intentionally and effectively mentor and model generosity to children. The church also has a wonderful opportunity to support those parents who yearn to help their children develop healthy values about money.

Parents, grandparents, tutors at afterschool programs, neighbors, and Sunday school teachers all have opportunities to be exemplars and witnesses to the joy of sharing. Most parents want their children to have healthy lives and grounded values. Parents want their children to grow up with values of compassion and kindness. However, many parents feel lacking in either the skills or the support needed to teach their children these values. A lack of skills is not a denial of the yearning within the heart of the parent. It is imperative that generous church people care enough to take the time to enrich the lives of children. Some children have parents who do not model generosity or impress the children by the example of their sharing. Churches can reach out to those families to help the entire family constellation find the joy of sharing and giving. Lives can be enriched!

Spiritual Connections

Church teaching reinforces parental training and modeling. Few of the participants in this study named the church as the most significant formative factor in their generosity. Those few who did were all people who pointed to adult experiences and training rather than childhood modeling. Nonetheless, the church has a valuable supportive role in nurturing the generosity of most giving people.

Regardless of the roots of a person's generosity, generous givers who channel substantial parts (or all) of their giving through the church usually express a connection with God through their giving. The connection is described in many different ways. The giver rarely articulates a systematic theological basis for his or her giving. Nevertheless, generous givers perceive that the giving is related to what God has done in their lives, is doing in their lives, or will do in their lives. The fact that they may be clumsy in their attempt to articulate *why* does not diminish the reality of the connection.

I am also convinced that some people have the spiritual gift of generosity as described in Paul's letter to the Romans (12:8). The need and desire to give generously is part of who they are. They find great spiritual satisfaction in sharing what they have and who they are. This spiritual gift is not reserved for any particular economic category. Church leaders can affirm the gift of generosity in all those who have it. Jesus upheld the action of a poor widow as she placed two coins in a Temple offering box. He also ate with fairly well-to-do people like Zacchaeus, who gave away large sums.

Generous givers give either in recognition of a relationship to God or as a means to reach out to God with whatever is important to them. Generosity is a heart response. It is not a calculated decision.

Ritual is an important aspect of church life. Even nonliturgical churches follow patterns. They have established ways of doing things. Ritual can be an aid to spiritual growth. Often, ritual begins before its meaning is evident. For many people, the ritual of church giving started long before they had any clear understanding of God or appreciation for the church. Never underestimate the power of ritual!

Christianity is not a solitary religion. The Holy Spirit comes upon the gathered people ("Where two or three are gathered in my name . . ."). The relationship of God is almost always experienced within the context of a community of faith. The faith community raises the issue of generosity and reinforces the inner compulsion to respond with both heart and purse. When giving is within the faith community, the relationship with God and others is informed and solidified.

The Connection With Others

A question might be whether Yahweh is a God who gives people responsibility to care for the creation, or whether giving is solely between the individual giver and God. Most generous people believe that they can make a difference in this world. They believe that their giving is related to God and to God's creation. They describe giving in relational terms. For some, the relationship is seen most clearly within the gathered community where they worship (and give). Others have a more all-encompassing understanding of God's people—some of whom they will never meet. I am convinced that the relationship of the giver to God and the relationship of the giver to others is part of one seamless garment.

Three biblical passages come to mind to express this connection. The first is the Great Commandment (Matthew 22:34-40). In that dramatic confrontation with the pharisaic lawyer, Jesus affirmed the connection between love of God and love of neighbor. The second passage is three chapters later in Matthew's account. In the parable of the Last Judgment, Jesus said, "Just as you did it to one of the least of these who are members of my family, you did it to me" (Matthew 25:40). Another blunt connection is found in the Epistle of James. The writer stated that we cannot claim to have faith if we are not willing to care for the person who is without food and clothing (James 2:14-17).

Giving also means a connection with others all around the globe. The eighteenth-century British priest John Wesley said, "I look upon all the world as my parish."[1] Wesley would not allow people to get away with claiming that the only people they are to care about are family members and the people who live next door. Many generous givers yearn to connect with people in their community and in other parts of the world who need food, clothing, and something safe to drink. They do not limit generosity to kinship ties or to their circle of friends.

Generational differences emerge in matters of relationships and connections. Many of the older people describe their relationship with God in the same language as they speak of their relationship to the church. That symbiotic connection between the spiritual dimension of giving and the institutional church is less common among younger people. They may greatly appreciate the loving support they receive from other people at the church, but it is not a primary factor. It is seen as supportive rather than essential.

Spiritual connections within the congregation may not be the primary factors that initiate giving, but they are essential in supporting the spiritual dimension of giving. There is a connection between the generous people of God and the faith community. People have influence upon one another—for good or for ill. Generosity begets generosity!

Many generous givers experience hostility from others for the faith and values they express in their day-to-day living. Other generous givers are ignored by others. When they come into the worshiping community, they are reminded that they are not alone in the struggle. They remember who they are and why they give. Most givers recognize that they could spend what they give rather than giving it away. Their giving affirms a different set of values from those of the secular world. The church has an opportunity each week to reinforce those values.

Research from the Independent Sector in Washington, DC, indicates that the people who give the most money to an organization are the people who volunteer the most time to the organization.[2] Their research does not make a distinction between church giving and other charitable giving. Although their studies make no attempt to draw a parallel between the giving of the people and their individual or family outreach, there is no reason to doubt that the correlation generally holds. Those who are most involved in the life and ministry of the congregation tend to be the most generous.

Throughout the Scriptures, givers are encouraged to give themselves as well as their money. Prophets railed against those who used their giving as insulation from God and against those who ignored the hurting in the world. Giving is to symbolize and grow out of a relationship rather than to become an excuse to keep from establishing healthy relationships.

Relationships don't just happen. They must be nurtured. No one plants today and harvests tomorrow. Just as the grain goes through a series of processes to mature, so also the route is long and convoluted for humans to become generous givers. No one little action, motivating speech, or lesson is sufficient. The example of a giving person is important, but it is not enough. Head stuff is important, but the heart has to be involved as well.

Soil has to be fertile for grain to produce a crop. But that is not enough. The soil must be prepared. Weeds have to be controlled. The seeds lie fallow in the ground for a period of time before they sprout. Water and nutrients are essential at every phase of growth.

THE KINGDOM OF GOD IS AS IF SOMEONE WOULD SCATTER SEED ON THE GROUND, AND WOULD SLEEP AND RISE NIGHT AND DAY, AND THE SEED WOULD SPROUT AND GROW, HE DOES NOT KNOW HOW. THE EARTH PRODUCES OF ITSELF, FIRST THE STALK, THEN THE HEAD, THEN THE FULL GRAIN IN THE HEAD. BUT WHEN THE GRAIN IS RIPE, AT ONCE HE GOES IN WITH HIS SICKLE, BECAUSE THE HARVEST HAS COME. (MARK 4:26-29)

I LIKE TO WORK IN MY YARD. WHEN SOMETHING IS PLANTED, I TEND TO KEEP WATCHING FOR A WHILE TO SEE IF IT IS COMING UP. THEN I GET INVOLVED IN OTHER THINGS AND FORGET TO WATCH. ALL OF A SUDDEN, I NOTICE THAT THE PLANTS ARE THROUGH THE GROUND—AND HAVE BEEN UP FOR A WHILE BUT I HAD NOT NOTICED.

So, too, leaders need to be aware that the absence of instant results does not signal a lack of something going on within a person or a community of faith. We may not notice any difference until all of a sudden we become aware that something has been happening in the lives of some people. Whenever growth emerges, we have the responsibility to cultivate and nurture it so that it may move on to maturity. The Holy Spirit operates on God's timetable, not ours.

The grain's nature is to produce seed. In much the same way, generous givers see themselves as giving, sharing people. It is part of who they are. Most of them were affirmed in that identity as children. Some came to that identity through affirmation and learning in a small group such as *Disciple* Bible study or a Covenant Discipleship Group. Whether they grew up seeing themselves as giving and sharing or came to that identity later in life, the church affirms that identity through its teachings and actions.

Self-Fulfillment and Giving

Generous giving is related to one's self-identity. For many generous people, giving helps them to be what they are—what God intended them to be. There are two primary identity factors that relate to generosity. One is the identity of the person as an individual. Am I a generous person or not? The second is the identity of the person within the community. Is my fulfillment found and expressed within a group of people who relate their life to Jesus of Nazareth, who gave his life for me and for all humankind?

Generous people do not see giving as a burden but rather as a matter of values and priorities. Giving reflects and witnesses to what is important in their lives. Generous Christians take their cues about life from the spirit of Jesus Christ rather than from the attractive seduction of television commercials. They place greater value on long-term issues than on the thrill of the moment. Generous Christians remember who they are. They are related to the God who is love. Their identity is connected to the One who gave his life that all might live abundantly. Through the living of their lives, each one affirms that his or her own life is also more abundant.

It is the responsibility of the church to help people discover their gifts in the first place, whatever those gifts may be. Secondly, the church has a responsibility to nurture the gifts as they are discovered. In some cases, people need training and information about how to use their gifts. After all, we are called to responsible use of the gifts for the building up of the church (Ephesians 4:16).

Even an individual spiritual gift cannot be expressed in complete isolation. It is to be developed and expressed within a community of faith. Many of the generous givers talked about the ways in which their giving was part of a corporate faith community called a congregation. They were not in this giving experience alone; they were part of a community of giving people. They were part of something bigger than themselves. Enthusiasm for the work of the church was described in many ways, but it was a common theme of the people I interviewed.

Racial-ethnic congregations provide a special kind of identity for the people within them. It was obvious from the interviews I conducted with Korean Christians that the Korean culture plays an important part in the identity of Korean Christians.

Hispanic Christians that I interviewed expressed a sense that they want to be self-supporting as congregations. It is an identity they are striving to have within the life of their denomination rather than something they have already attained.

African American givers seemed to express joy in giving in a way that is rarely seen in other North American congregations. Whether they were rich or poor, there was a sense of affirmation and joy expressed through their giving—a joy in the goodness of the Lord.

Native Americans seemed to have the most holistic view of giving and sharing. It encompassed sharing with the whole universe, not just money and not only with other people.

The Church as Community

"The institutional church" is not a dirty word in my experience. Faith without structures is like a body without bones or a house without joists and rafters. For all of its faults, we need the church. Jesus founded a real church with imperfect people.

Perhaps an analogy will help. There is much about the government of my nation that irritates and sometimes infuriates me. The alternative is not to get rid of government. A lack of governmental structure results in anarchy. We have to have structure in our nation. Some dependable method is required to establish standards for commerce, to adjudicate disputes, and to develop infrastructure. Without structure there is chaos.

In addition to the pragmatic requirements of a civil society, the nation helps define who we are. It gives us identity. No matter how inept or corrupt a government is, the citizens of most countries are proud to be known as (fill in the name of the country). Our national identity is part of who we are.

In the same manner, the visible, sin-tainted church has been and is now an important part of my life. The church nurtured me from my infancy and educated me in her institutions. The institutional church, with additional assistance from my wife, has economically supported me for all my adult life. During times of sadness, the people who are part of the institutional church sustained me through prayer and encouragement. Sometimes they called me to greater accountability by forcing my attention onto my own shortcomings and sins. There are many things good and right about the church. It is part of the identity of the people interviewed for this book.

However, I am acutely aware that there are also many things wrong with the church. The ways it has dealt with money issues have rarely been helpful. In the first place, churches hardly ever provide guidance and counsel about the values that undergird all spending, saving, and giving decisions. Secondly, at the time of the annual giving campaign, faith is often interpreted as a way to get healthier, wealthier, and wiser. In many, many congregations, the campaign is followed by total silence about money for the next eleven months.

Contemporary people are easily mesmerized by the American dream and forget the dream of a new heaven and a new earth. Church people are not immune to those temptations. Church people can place their identity in the institution rather than in the presence of God with the people of God.

All of us discover ourselves seduced by concerns for our own well-being while ignoring the cries of those with hunger, fear, and oppression. Church leaders find it too easy to become wrapped up in building institutions instead of proclaiming the justice and mercy of God. This is part of the lovers' quarrel that I continue to have with a church I deeply love. It is a confession of my own complicity.

Scriptural abundance is defined by relationships rather than by accumulation. It has more to do with quality of life than with quantity of things. Generous people care more about people than they do about "stuff." Generous people have discovered the joy of sharing and discarded the burden of amassing.

Generous people do not claim exemption from temptation. They are not perfect. They like things too. I did not interview any generous people who asserted that material things are automatically sinful. Whether rich or poor, whether Euro-American, African American, Hispanic, Asian, or Native American, they enjoyed being part of the western economic world. They were fully a part of their communities, and they wanted to be a participating part in the culture.

In the best of all possible giving worlds, the gift is a response to the one who forgives us of our sins and seeks abundant life for us. Paul stated the connection in his letter to the Corinthians (2 Corinthians 8:9). Paul tied the collection both to the act of God through Jesus Christ and the need of the people for whom the collection was intended. It is not an either-or. The giver, the recipient, and God are all part of the equation. It is our task as leaders of the church to help people see, experience, and name the connection.

The Role of the Church

Unless people see themselves as part of the body (a branch on the vine), their giving will only represent the support of an institution to meet their personal psychological and social needs but not necessarily participation in the ministry of Christ in this world. Ego-centered giving is not an expression of the new being in Christ. Another vital dimension of community is illustrated in the Gospel story of Jesus' encounter with the man in the cemetery (Mark 5:1-20). The crazed man said his name was Legion. Legion signified the powerful forces that had such a disastrous effect over him. There are many principalities and powers in every culture that seek to entice us to live by a different set of

THERE IS A DIFFERENCE BETWEEN PAYING FOR SERVICES AND SHARING IN MINISTRY. THE FIRST KEEPS THE INSTITUTION GOING SO THAT MY NEEDS ARE MET. THE SECOND UNITES PEOPLE IN CHRIST'S MISSION IN THE WORLD.

plumb lines than the justice, mercy, and love shown in the life, death, and resurrection of Jesus of Nazareth. It is tough to fight the battle alone. We need a faith community that strengthens and supports us and lovingly holds us accountable to exhibit the fruit of the Spirit in our day-to-day lives.

Walking the Walk

Throughout the Bible, the Word of God and the acts of God are intertwined. Moses not only heard God calling him but also saw the burning bush. The prophets did not simply speak the prophetic word but enacted it (see Jeremiah 19, Isaiah 20, Ezekiel 4–5, and Hosea). Their actions were symbolic in the fullest sense of that word. The Word became flesh in their actions.[3]

> *I WILL PUT MY LAW WITHIN THEM, AND I WILL WRITE IT ON THEIR HEARTS; AND I WILL BE THEIR GOD, AND THEY SHALL BE MY PEOPLE.*
>
> *(JEREMIAH 31:33)*

Financial giving is an enactment, a visible sign of devotion. Jesus took bread, broke it, and gave it to the disciples as he spoke to them of his self-giving. Just as the act and the word were often part of one movement in the Scriptures, so generous givers do not simply say that they love God. They give in order to demonstrate (enact) their devotion. For many of these people, the visible word of their giving is done not to witness to others but as part of their quiet response to the prior Word (and activity) of God in their lives.

This is an argument for putting more drama into the gathering and dedication of the funds that are given. The liturgical acts may be used as an excuse, but there is little relational giving without liturgy. We want giving to be more than a wise transaction—with either the IRS or with God. It is part of worship, and worship needs to be enacted as well as spoken.

Many people have observed that Jesus said more about money than he did about any other subject except the reign of God. All through the Hebrew Bible, we find references to the faithful (and unfaithful) use of money and property. If those who preach will face the economic and value-centered issues of these passages rather than spiritualizing all the earthly dimensions of the passages, a major step will have been taken to help people see the connection between giving and worship.

Sometimes our lives encounter God in ways we hardly recognize, as in the stories of Jacob in Genesis 28 through 32. When Jacob dreamed about the angels on the ladder and the promise of God, he responded by making a commitment to reorder his economic life (Genesis 28:20-22). Later, when Jacob wrestled with a man at Peniel, he recognized what had happened only after the experience (Genesis 32:22-30); but he continued to change his life as a result of the encounter.

The prophets described the suffering that Israel caused God. They told the stories not to make the people wallow in guilt or feel sorry for God but to get the nation to repent—to change its direction. Likewise, our appeal to people to give is not in order to get people to feel sorry for God or for the church. It is not even for people to do good unto others. It is for the church to help people relate to God in a mutually helpful manner. As long as our focus is on accumulation rather than relationships (with God and with others), there can be little growth or joy in giving. God calls us to care for God's creatures so that good happens through our lives of giving.

Locating the Leverage Points

Financial leaders in congregations often complain that their church has a wealthy member who contributes virtually nothing to support the church's ministry. Sometimes, church leaders complain that the rich member gives lots of money away, but it is all given to other institutions. The church (at least, their congregation) receives none of it.[4]

Perhaps the reason many wealthy people fail to give large gifts to their church is that their church has not dreamed big enough to capture the imagination of these potential donors. Many large donors want to make a difference in the world. They may not be convinced that the church has a big enough heart or a big enough dream to make a difference.

Most of the people who attend our North American churches are middle class. We have not done a good job of reaching the poor or the rich. Financial problems in the church will not likely be solved by learning how to get money from wealthy individuals or from foundations. Spending our time on getting money from the wealthy can be an escape mechanism that does not face up to our own calling to be giving people.

From the beginning of the church in the first century of the common era, congregations have consisted primarily of ordinary people. Paul could say to the young church in Corinth, "Not many of you were wise by human standards, not many were powerful, not many were of noble birth" (1 Corinthians 1:26). That is still true today. Neither new methodologies for getting money from the wealthy or foundations nor better campaign materials is the answer.

One important claim in this book is that church leaders made a fundamental error when we decided that the financial problems of the church are primarily methodological. We easily assumed that better curriculum in the Sunday school and more dynamic giving-campaign materials are the answer to financial difficulties in the church. However, opinions vary about the quality of curriculum. What are reasonable expectations for curriculum? And if the answer to the financial problems were effective campaign materials, our problem should have already been solved by the wide variety of campaign programs available on the North American market.

Another current target of blame is the seminary. Spiritual leaders among the laity are often aghast to discover that seminaries rarely offer courses to address issues of personal finance, church budget building, funding counsel, or financial management. If a course that addresses stewardship theology is offered, it seldom connects the theology to the day-to-day realities of funding the ministry of the congregation.

Seminary faculty are more likely to speak disparagingly of denominations than they are to present an apologetic for connectional ministry. Most of all, anything to do with either personal or institutional finances seems beneath the standards of the academy.

Some of my colleagues in denominational stewardship offices believe that the problem would be solved if we could get a stewardship chair in each of the seminaries. I doubt it. It isn't that simple. Sound stewardship theology is important. Raising money is an essential part of a parish and denominational operation in our day. Good tools are essential to the tasks. I question, though, whether the seminary is the best setting to provide these essential parts of the total picture. I also question whether the seminary experience is a "teachable moment" in the lives of most seminarians.

My conclusion is that curriculum, financial campaign materials, and seminary training are all important, but the lack thereof is not the core problem. In fact, there are two core problems. First, we have tried to build a house on sand. The house isn't bad; it simply doesn't have a solid foundation. Second, we do not see giving as part of the way God has provided to help people grow in their relationship with God and with one another.

Just as the culture has separated economics from religion, we have acted as though funding the ministry of the church has little to do with faith. We have adopted all the best secular fundraising methods available. They are not bad, but they are not the primary issue. We have studied psychology and sociology to craft more skillful methods. Knowledge of people and the culture are vitally important for effective communication, but they are not the end all and be all. A few good books are available on stewardship theology. The ability to explain our theological position may be affirming, but it is rarely converting. Unfortunately, we have failed to communicate to one another that sharing of our resources is a basic part of commitment to Jesus Christ. All of these disciplines put together are not as crucial as the transforming power of the Holy Spirit working in the midst of a group of seeking people.

Even those who have felt that giving is a faith issue tend to look for the *right* stewardship theology. The theological approach is rational to the point of being rationalistic. The problem is that people do not reason their way into giving—even when their reasoning starts with theology. Decisions about giving, spending, and keeping are emotional and heart issues. They come from the center of the person rather than from the edges.

In the church we often talk about giving "off the top." By that, we mean that those who wait until the end of the pay period to give generously rarely have anything left to give. Those who write the church check at the beginning of the month are much more likely to feel better about their giving and to give more. Quite often the rationale is based on Paul's advice to the Corinthians: "On the first day of every week, each of you is to put aside and save whatever extra you earn, so that collections need not be taken when I come" (1 Corinthians 16:2). When the Scriptures are used in this way, we are urged to give off the top because it is so rational to do so.

Most of us are subject to cultural blindness or egoistic myopia. We repeatedly fail to challenge many of the assumptions we live with. We allow our identity to be shaped by advertisers rather than by the Spirit of God and the community of faith. That failure continuously creates long-term problems.

Finding fulfillment in one part of life is not possible without finding fulfillment in all of life. Church leaders and church members in North America are part of a culture that segments life into tiny compartments then builds walls between the compartments. I do not accuse the church of being the builder of the walls, but the church seems to have adopted the architecture. Observers bewail the loss of community in individualized North America. A spirit of being part of one another is often missing in many of our churches. Rather than dissecting the past, God calls us to focus our efforts on building a loving and just community for the future.

For clergy, the spoken word is much more likely to communicate if it is related to acts that are both liturgical and instrumental. Many clergy dutifully preach the annual stewardship sermon in the fall of the year. For a variety of reasons, most pastors resent the obligation. I doubt that these sermons make much of an impact. In fact, they tend to support the idea that money and religion have nothing in common. The annual stewardship campaign comes across as an interruption in the spiritual life of the congregation rather than being integral to it.

When the people in the pews have such a wide variety of stories, it is difficult to communicate one message that will find a place to settle in each person. The responsibility of leadership is to help church members and churchgoers identify themselves as people loved by God with such assurance that they are free to express that identity in their daily life.

When the Playing Field Is Not Even

A person who believes that he or she has nothing to give is miserable. Generosity is not a matter of large gifts but of proportionality. In fact, many poor people are generous, giving people. Middle-class and wealthy folks are often amazed to discover that poor people believe that they have something to give. Poor people give generously because they don't try to give what they don't have; they give what they do have. Many affluent people have their eyes and hearts fixed on what they do not have and therefore think that they have nothing to give.

Individuals with the ability to give are not the only ones who fail to live up to their God-given potential. Congregations can be caught up in status and power as well. Churches face a dilemma whenever they build or redecorate. How fancy should the addition be? Should we spend $100,000 on a new kitchen when the same amount of money would provide one hundred wells with clean water for African villages? Should we put a big-screen television in the youth room of the new family center when there are children within two miles of the church who go without a healthy meal most days?

WHY IS IT THAT ONE PERSON WITH A CLOSET FULL OF CLOTHES THINKS HE HAS NOTHING TO GIVE, WHILE ANOTHER PERSON WILL GIVE YOU THE SHIRT OFF HIS BACK?

The decisions are complicated by the story of the woman who broke a jar of costly perfume and used it to anoint the feet of Jesus (Mark 14:3-9). How do we balance this story of extravagance with Jesus' word to the wealthy young man to sell everything and give it to the poor (Mark 10:17-31)? Is a gift for a new chapel more generous that a sandwich given to a hungry street person?

What is the church's responsibility to proclaim justice in a nation where there are great inequities? When a system locks people into abject poverty, the whole system is in need of repentance. The system needs to be changed along with individual hearts. Does generosity include the giving of skill and energy to change broken systems? How are these skills affirmed?

How can churches become a humanizing force in the communities where they are located on our planet? When Jesus said that he came that people may have life abundantly, the abundant life certainly included more than financial riches. Many people with wealth fail to live abundantly, though it is very difficult for a person to live abundantly while lacking the basic necessities of life.

Fundraising Verses Faith Raising

Our task is to cooperate with the work of the Holy Spirit to invite, nurture, and encourage people into holistic faith. Holistic life is seen in the person of Jesus, who gave himself for others. Wholeness is different from "finding our center." It is turning outward rather than inward. It is love in action. Giving and sharing are integral parts of that journey toward wholeness that is love.

Endnotes

1 From "Journal from August 12, 1738, to November 1, 1739," by John Wesley.

2 See *Giving and Volunteering in the United States: Findings from a National Survey* (Independent Sector, 1996); page 5.

3 I do not intend to imply that financial giving is comparable to the symbolic acts or forceful words of the prophets. The analogy must not be taken too far.

4 A deficiency of this study is that I did not talk to anyone who would be considered very rich. Several years before this research began, I interviewed a man who gave $80,000 to his local church and put an additional $80,000 per year into the church's endowment fund. He hoped that he could put enough in before he died to continue the level of his giving. Nor did I ask people if they included the church in their estate planning. That issue will have to wait for another study.

Personal Epilogue

Back to the Beginning

I t is easy to get seduced into the pragmatic principalities and powers that surround us in North American institutional religion. The interviews became a transformational experience for me. Even though I spent years emphasizing that giving is a spiritual issue rather than a fundraising technique, I admit I hoped to discover techniques. This study did not end up where I anticipated. It may not have ended where you, the reader, anticipated either.

If you bought this book looking for magic formulas for church fundraising, you did not find what you were looking for. Instead, you discovered conversations. I ended up with stories instead of rules. If this study had proved that there are seven steps for increasing giving, this book would sell like hotcakes; but it would not have been honest.

It is evident that people give for a complex conglomeration of reasons. In these interviews, people told stories to talk about their reasons for giving. Most of the stories were rooted in childhood experiences, but that is not the whole story. Older people often described a church experience that took place during their childhood. Young adults were more apt to speak of a family influence unrelated to church. Older people almost always related giving money. Younger people generally placed more emphasis on the generosity of time.

In almost every case, the sustaining and supporting message of the Scriptures discovered in the presence of a small group or a worshiping community helped people connect their early experiences with adult decisions. The issue is not whether the key is the family or the church. Each needs the other. Each can contribute to the other.

You may gather different insights than I did from reading the stories of the people. That is not only okay; it is desirable. Stories have many dimensions. In fact, it is wonderful if you made some fresh discoveries in listening to the words of the people who told their stories to me. More importantly, I hope you have recalled your own stories as you have read the stories of the interviewees. I hope that church leaders will do far more listening to the people in their congregations and communities.

Asking questions is more important than learning facts. Stories are more important than data. We can pour over all sorts of statistical data and never connect people to the Source of all life. There is a danger that our hunger for facts, data, and information is a hunger for power. We have all heard that knowledge is power. Do we want to know facts in order to coerce people into doing what we want, or is our primary concern to connect people with people and help all the people connect with the Almighty?

Conversations are more important than conclusions. Relationships are of greater value than meeting a budget.

The Real Bottom Line

If you read this book in order to learn how to get more money out of folks, I hope you don't remember a thing from it. If you read the book and learned something about your own relationship to God, my writing it was worth the effort. If you are a leader in a church and you learned something about how to affirm the generosity of giving people, and if you got a glimpse of a way to help people who seek a personal relationship with God, then my effort in writing the book is vindicated. The bottom line is that giving is a faith issue rather than a fundraising issue.

Today's conclusions will probably not be appropriate tomorrow. Contexts change. Your own stories profoundly affect the way you will act in the future. Stories help you know who you are. Perhaps the stories told in this book will help you recall some of your own stories.

Listening to the stories of people who are finding or have found fulfillment in life is a more helpful way of learning about the abundant life than talking to folks who feel that their lives are a waste. There seems little evidence that "more, more, more" brings happiness and fulfillment. The generous people who told me their stories are folks who have discovered an alternative center in their lives. They have grounded their lives in giving rather than in accumulating. Through these conversations, I am convinced that identity is the most important factor in giving.

I don't agree with the dictum that "if people's hearts get right, the money will come." Jesus put it the reverse way when he said, "Where your treasure is, there your heart will be also" (Matthew 6:21). At least those who think that a godly heart will produce funds for the ministries of the church see that there is a connection between one's money and one's relationship with the Almighty. Unfortunately, many church leaders do not even believe that there is a correlation. They want to get the heart of the person connected to God, and then they come along with secular fundraising techniques that divorce money and giving. That is part of the problem in our culture.

When money is separated from God, money becomes the god. Again, it was Jesus who said, "No one can serve two masters" (Matthew 6:24). We have tried to have it both ways. It didn't work in Jesus' time, and it will not work today. We have only one life to live. Money is essential to human survival in the present world; that does not mean that money is God. Unless money is harnessed for the glory of God, it becomes a straightjacket that keeps us from walking with God. It is that simple. Help people find the joy of keeping all things in perspective. So be it. Amen.

Final Actions on the Basis of This Book

1. If your church received fifty percent more money this year than was anticipated when the budget was developed, what would be done with the extra money? Your answer says a lot about your understanding of the mission of the church—regardless of what the congregation's mission statement says.

2. The next time you are tempted to send someone from your committee to a stewardship seminar, save your money and have the people who would have gone invest an equivalent amount of time listening to people in your congregation tell their personal stories of giving.

Post your responses to these actions on the stewardship web page at www.gbod.org/stewardship/.